Out of Eden

Out of Eden

The Eden Project Companion

eden project | books

Contents

Health 138

Materials 178

Out of Eden 224

Into Eden

Down at the tip of Cornwall, in the south-west of the UK, a group of people decided to build a global garden in a china clay pit: a pit that had no soil, no level ground and was 15 metres below the water table. Why? To demonstrate that regeneration (both social and environmental) was possible, that people with very different skills could work together to produce something greater than the sum of their parts, to reconnect people with nature, to encourage people to look at their world with fresh eyes and most importantly to explore possible positive futures. They called it the Eden Project.

This book is not about the Eden Project so much as about the themes and ideas that we represent through our exhibits and events. It is about what Eden is about. The displays we have created are not attempts to re-create functioning fragments of nature, and they are certainly not an exercise in what is known as 'ex situ conservation' (keeping rare and endangered plants safe in artificial environments). There are places that have specialized in being world class at these activities (Biosphere Two in Arizona in the first case; the Millennium Seed Bank at Wakehurst Place, West Sussex, in the second). Eden's goals were simply to produce combinations of plants, landscape design and art that reflected the real diversity of the world, to remind us how much wonder there is in the world and how dependent we are on those natural resources. What we present at Eden is therefore a bit like a view of the world through a train window. Places are glimpsed, sometimes too briefly, as you move past and through the landscape, but perhaps you will see enough detail to so intrigue you that one day you will explore them, or their stories, in more detail.

The rice exhibit in the Humid Tropics Biome

> *'The trouble with our times is that the future is not what it used to be.'*   Paul Valéry

But it would be a mistake to present the Eden gardens as simply a passive diorama – we wanted to deliver an experience that was sufficiently dramatic and complex to evoke the sense of really being in whatever part of the world was being represented. Maybe you have to squint just a little, but stand in the giant Mediterranean conservatory – the Warm Temperate Biome – and breathe in the smells of rosemary and lavender, and see the cistus flowering on the terraces, and just for a moment you can feel yourself on a Spanish hillside.

And although the displays are facsimiles, they go beyond simply being a homage because they have the beauty of a garden. The plants are real and have their own amazing textures, patterns, colours and scents; the architecture has often, rightly, been described as having a cathedral quality; and the art found throughout the landscapes, indoors and out, abounds with the creative energy of the many talented people who have contributed ideas.

The Tropic Trader, symbol of world trade, greets visitors

Each of the individual exhibits has a theme. Many refer to a particular part of the world and depict land uses and the plants that are typical of that region. Others focus on particular plants and commodities or plant-based products, such as coffee, cocoa or fibres. It is these themes that are explored in this book, within overarching categories of biodiversity, food, health and materials.

The Malaysian exhibit in the Humid Tropics Biome re-creates a forest farmer's productive garden

Above: *The pit at Bodelva, as found*

Below: *Picasso meets the Aztecs in the contour landscaping...*

14

One very important plant zone is missing here, the dry tropics, one third of the world's land surface. There people live on the edge of existence, adapting, as do plants, to the lack of water. In the first phase of building Eden we did not have enough money to develop a Dry Tropics Biome as well, but we still hope to see it one day. It will provide the missing piece of the jigsaw of plants and people – a vital piece, because 25 per cent of the world's population live in these regions, and they comprise half of the land surface of the world's developing countries, where crop failure can mean disaster.

The fact that the site we used for doing all this was a china clay pit coming to the end of its working life is of course an important part of the Eden Project story. It is one thing to build a garden to display the diversity and riches of the world, but doing so in the large, soil-less rainwater-sump that was Bodelva was probably one of the biggest horticultural challenges ever undertaken. Very often botanic gardens are set up on derelict or poor land, usually because better land is nabbed for agricultural crops. The Royal Botanic Gardens, Kew, are on Thames alluvium and a frost plain, and are a good precedent for creating something of enduring worth in unpromising conditions. Nobody, however, has created a world-class garden in such a steep-sided pit, and the techniques of soil manufacture and stabilization that we used are unique. Our gardeners have had to learn to abseil, sometimes planting while being 'roped-in'.

Visitors sometimes ask if Eden is a botanic garden. The answer is yes and no. Eden is primarily an educational project, and the status of education has often slipped down the agendas of many traditional botanic gardens, although all the European examples started as teaching gardens. Eden also displays crops throughout the site: not single specimens for demonstration purposes but at field scale (or at least chunks of fields). We do this to encourage our visitors to remember that not only are the plants vital for us but also that somebody, somewhere, has to grow them. Acquiring the plants for this has involved researching cultigens (plant species or varieties known only in cultivation) and landraces (primitive or antique varieties usually associated with traditional agriculture, and often highly adapted to local conditions) in the world's gene banks – something that most UK botanic gardens have not done since they were government agencies researching potential economic crops for Britain and the Empire.

Eden is unconstrained by the government or university links of many of Europe's botanical gardens. It is also not encumbered by having to maintain listed buildings (although it is doubtless only a matter of time before some of our architecture is listed!). That means we can turn our face resolutely to the future, to local issues as well as global issues, to the use of plants as resources, just as many new botanic gardens in developing countries are doing. And this is what drives our plant displays: they have a 'development focus'.

Many great gardens have had significant designers involved in their layout, working with formality, sightlines, scale, a balance of intimate and public space and so on. So too has Eden. Dominic Cole of Land Use Consultants was faced with the huge challenge of creating a landscape appropriate to Eden's remit: not the gorse and birch appropriate to a Cornish clay pit but a landscape of human use of plants containing over eighty themed exhibits. Inspired partly by the patternation of allotments and the need for land stabilization, he created large swathes of planting reminiscent of contour ploughing, a unique vision of land use. Part of the horticultural challenge at Eden has been to realize this vision in such details as alignment. This is difficult to do in a pit where drainage is often hard to predict, where springs appear and disappear, and where, for example, one section of a hedge line dies off because of impeded drainage while another area thrives. Dominic remains the overall authority on aesthetic layout at the project, and is the horticultural equivalent of the Biome architects.

Construction of the Biomes well under way in 2000

17

The judgement of many professional horticulturists visiting Eden in its first year was that the horticulture was rough around the edges. The pressure of delivering the Project showed, and therefore the emphasis moved to improving horticultural standards, retrofitting deficient landscape details and delivering horticultural excellence. Eden was also affected by a national problem: the lack of practical skills among horticulturists, caused by centuries of low pay and low status. Determined to turn this around, Eden soon became a market leader in pay and conditions and increased its horticultural workforce. The emphasis from the beginning has been to recruit people with local knowledge of floras from around the world, agroforestry knowledge and experience of local crops. The staff also began to take international trainees as capacity allowed and to recruit staff from overseas, a deviation from the usual Eden policy of recruiting primarily from Cornwall.

At Eden we see a much wider spectrum of visitors than most public gardens, including people who have never really stopped to consider that a plant is alive, thought of them as a resource or linked them in any way to their everyday lives. Our style of interpretation obviously strikes a chord, but these audiences also need plant drama. Temporary displays are important, not only in the Warm Temperate Biome, where crops are removed in autumn, creating large gaps, but whenever an opportunity presents itself. Showmanship – building on the popularity of flower shows – is now an established part of Eden's horticultural style and a vital way of attracting the return visitor. Whenever you come there is something new to see.

Horticulturists work closely with all the Eden teams. The Green Team work with the Education and Arts Teams on exhibit planning. This cross-disciplinary approach successfully enlists

The Eden nursery at Watering Lane

interpretative ideas to create innovative displays and is certainly one of the approaches that differentiate Eden from other horticultural attractions.

The Eden nursery When the nursery was acquired at the beginning of October 1997, it was the only home for the gestation of the Eden Project, and so it had to serve as a base for all the planning and a site from which to launch requests for funding. There was never any opposition to getting started with growing plants, even if there was a decided shortage of money with which to do so – building Eden and having no plants to put in it was a much greater worry – and the feeling was that, if we were to impress donors, showing visitors that we were already on the road to filling those Biomes was a good way to tell donors that we were in this for real.

Trying to work miracles with tropical plants so far from their natural habitat involved more than a little bravado, as we had to learn how to grow the plants, and not surprisingly we learnt how *not* to grow some of them. Yet another reason to be grateful that nature has provided us with so many species of plant was that if we had yet to learn how to grow one particular species, well, there was another that would do the job that we could grow successfully.

We have often been asked about our travels to distant lands to hunt out the plants we grew on in the nursery, something that is now increasingly uncommon as botanic gardens struggle with the legal obstacles to plant acquisition presented by the Convention on Biological Diversity. Strange that even the most avid gardeners should assume that this was what we did, for actually we did what many a gardener has done when faced with an empty plot, namely visit friends and admire their plants. Sure as grass pollen gets up the nose we would return with cuttings, seeds and plants that we were

Olive trees ready for planting in the Warm Temperate Biome

19

assured were 'looking for a good home'. Our gardening friends might have been running botanical gardens, university research facilities and private gardens visited by thousands of people a year, but we all shared a love of plants. Also, right from the earliest days, offers came in from individuals who were no longer able to look after a much-loved plant. Sometimes this was just what we had been looking for; at other times we had the difficult task of explaining that we just couldn't accommodate yet another rubber plant or cactus.

The nursery was a major supplier for the plant collection before the full opening of the main site, but after that we had to redefine its role. Now the function of the nursery is to provide the right plants at the right time. Many of the plants we grow are short-lived. So growing annual crops and flowers for exhibits and display will continue to be one of the nursery's roles. This theme is continued with its role of growing plants for harvest, so that we can take the produce to the main site. This might be for out-of-season display, of, say, gourds or seed heads of cereals. It is also necessary to keep a range of plants in containers in the nursery so that they can be moved out for external events – agricultural shows and the like – and also to help promote events in the local community. But we can also use them at the main site for temporary beautification when we have speakers giving presentations; it is useful for cocoa growers from Ghana, for instance, to give their talk standing next to a young cocoa tree grown in the nursery. Close contact with living plants is one of the aims of the Eden Project.

Eden will continue to succeed by coming up with new horticultural ideas and developments, whether on new ground or to replace existing plantings that have served their purpose. So, beyond serving the need to keep a few reserves for the replacement of 'accidents', the nursery helps Eden to redefine itself, including trialling new plants or seed selections for the exhibits.

What *don't* we do at the nursery? Well, while we did achieve excellent rates of growth from seed, cuttings and young plants, there is no way that we could have achieved broad-diameter tree trunks that only come with years of development. So the largest trees for the main site were bought in, although they often spent a year or so getting their breath back being quarantined in the nursery, some having had all the soil washed from their roots. Where ornamental plants can be easily bought at the required stage on the open market, it has often made sense to do so, especially when they can be sourced locally. And we rarely grow plants specifically for sale in the shop, because we wish to encourage new suppliers. However, in a new initiative, we are developing crop protocols to enable local suppliers to grow for us to a high standard.

Plants at the nursery awaiting their turn in the limelight

Plant facts

Over the past five years we have built up an amazing plant collection at Eden, including some of the tallest, oldest, fastest growing and hungriest in the world. We have around 130,000 plants of around 3,500 species in total, though both numbers fluctuate seasonally due to the many different crops we grow throughout the year.

The Outdoor Biome is by far the largest area at the Eden Project, and boasts well over 100,000 plants, many of them in the mass plantings of single species which create such a dramatic effect, such as the avenue of blue agapanthus which leads you to the entrance of the Biomes, or the hedge made up of thousands of yew trees which winds along the path away from the Visitor Centre to the bottom of the pit.

Just as in nature, the Humid Tropics Biome has the highest plant diversity with around 1,500 different species. One of the tallest trees in the world is *Koompassia excelsa*, from Malaysia, which can reach 84 metres in height. This can be seen growing in the Malaysian area of the Humid Tropics Biomes, although it will still be a while yet before it reaches the Biome roof! The tallest tree in the Biome is the kapok tree (*Ceiba pentandra*), which is about 20 metres in height, though it can reach 70 metres in its native Tropical America and Africa.

In the Malaysian region of the Humid Tropics Biome we have the titan arum (*Amorphophallus titanum*) which has one of the biggest flowers in the world, up to 3 metres in diameter. It is also renowned for being one of the nastiest, smelling as it does of rotting flesh! The titan arum at Eden flowered in the spring of 2005. Also growing in the Malaysian area is the plant with the largest undivided leaf, the giant taro (*Alocasia macrorrhizos*) whose leaves can measure 3 metres by 2 metres.

The largest seed at Eden is the coco-de-mer (*Lodoicea maldivica*) endemic to the Seychelles. The seed, which can measure up to 50 centimetres and weigh 20 kilograms, takes many years to germinate.

The Warm Temperate Biome contains over 12,000 plants, including what are almost certainly the Project's oldest, the olive trees (*Olea europaea*) in the Mediterranean. Some of our olives are estimated to be around 150 years old.

The procurement of so many different plants for our Biomes has been a mammoth task, with over 400 different sources in 30 countries. Over 100 universities, research institutes and botanic gardens have donated plant material, and it is from these places that most of our rarer varieties have come. The rest have mainly come from nurseries around Europe and Britain – many of them in Cornwall. They have arrived in the form of seeds, bulbs, cuttings or mature plants and have been delivered in anything from small envelopes to articulated lorries.

Finally, and rather behind the scenes, there is the ongoing process of learning how to grow the plants even better, what pests they may have and be susceptible to, and how they perform in our conditions. On one level this is a practical, and legal, matter of quarantining both plants that have come from abroad and, for good measure, all plants that we accept. This is one of the most important aspects of the nursery's work; currently there is a long list of pathogens successfully intercepted, including pathogens 'notifiable' to the Plant Health and Seeds Inspectorate. This aside, we may also carry out further research on the plants or simply note how the plants we need to grow perform, keeping proper records for future reference as trial reports. The nursery also hosts a seed store and a small laboratory for testing seed viability, soil nutrients and some pathogens. This is particularly important for holding on to stocks of agricultural seed sourced from international gene banks and not easily re-ordered.

Chemical pesticides are a last resort at Eden

NO ENTRY

CHEMICAL TREATMENT!

CP15

22

Pest control

Pest control Like most Millennium projects, Eden was required to deliver on a short timescale. This was the source of many a horticultural challenge, particularly that of stocking the Biomes rapidly with mature, 'characterful' plants. Horticulturists know that these often perform less well in the long run, serving the function of nurse crops, while younger whips rush ahead full of seedling vigour. Instant gardening also brings the challenge of plant health problems, and Eden would not be spared.

One of the main problems is knowing exactly what is going on. How do you know if there is a spider mite infestation at the top of a 14-metre-high tree? How do you know where to do preventative fungicide treatments? Although we can plan in advance, biology is never predictable. Even after quarantine we have to inspect and monitor our plants on a regular basis, and on a site the size of Eden (not to mention the nursery) doing this has to be a team effort. Any significant problems are sent to our horticultural science team who makes the diagnoses and plan the treatments. All this information is put on a database to remind us each year of the problems we have had in the past. We also record the treatments that work and those that don't!

For hard-to-reach areas we have to be a bit more ingenious in how we monitor the plants. The horticultural staff regularly use a scissor lift to prune some of the larger trees, and this provides an opportunity to inspect the canopy. More high-tech options include using a very small lipstick-sized camera, which can be pushed into the tree canopy on a long stick and take close-up pictures of the plants and any bugs; and the Flybot, a radio-controlled airship with a camera mounted on it.

Once the bugs have been found we have to control them. Predatory insects are the first option. Biological control has been around since before the Second World War. The predatory mite (*Phytoseiulus persimilis*) was discovered by accident on a consignment of orchids from Chile. This mite was found to be an extremely voracious predator of the two-

Sulawesi white-eyes, tree frogs, mantids and geckos help to keep pests at bay in the Humid Tropics Biome

spotted spider mite (*Tetranychus urticae*), the bane of tomato and cucumber growers' lives. Next came *Encarsia formosa*, a parasitic wasp for whitefly. Once organophosphates were found to kill all known pests research into biocontrols took a back seat, but one of the many minus points of organophosphates was that spider mites were very quick to build up resistance to them, and soon the organophosphates were ineffective against them. So *Phytoseiulus* was rediscovered, and there has been no stopping the development of biological control agents since. There are at least three commercially available predators for spider mite, and a handful just for aphid control. We work closely with companies such as Biological Crop Protection, who produce our beneficial insects and give us advice on the best ways of

using them. In the Biomes we have also introduced other larger creatures, including birds, frogs and lizards, that help keep pest populations down. The animals came from Newquay Zoo and have been bred in captivity.

When there is a large population of pests a different strategy is needed. If the pest can be physically removed by cutting out the affected part of the plant or by changing the environmental conditions, the problem can be addressed quickly. If neither of these options is viable, we can always fall back on pesticides. We always opt first for the 'soft' contact chemicals such as oils and fatty acids, which are very similar to the washing-up liquids that are used at home. We also use new-style pesticides that are highly selective and integrate with the biological control agents that we use.

Art, science, education

Communication and education were always central to the original vision of Eden, and to these ends complex social, environmental and economic stories meet and inform each other through the tangible medium of plants. The Creative Team has developed an eclectic arts-based approach to interpretation that lends itself both to the diversity of stories and to the need to engage audiences on an emotional and intellectual level.

The key challenge was to develop a new language to demystify science and successfully engage a broad cross-section of visitors, from academics to amateur gardeners, and from committed environmentalists to inner-city schoolchildren. The team has been joined by an in-house team of storytellers, designer-makers, producers and production managers and has worked with hundreds of local – and, increasingly, international – artists to explore solutions to this challenge. Many of these relationships have become long term, with artists returning to create new work on an annual basis.

As the team developed its ideas, it became clear that there was exciting potential for Eden to become a great cultural as well as a great horticultural destination. Revolutionary landscape design, world-class horticulture, iconic architecture, cutting-edge engineering, innovative education and a distinctive approach to communication involving the visual and performing arts could combine to create a unique and powerful experience for its visitors. Eden has also been recognized as one of the most exciting and spectacular venues for live performance in the world.

The storytellers

The storytellers complement the art, sculpture, poetry and prose across the site. They tell tales of plants and people, myth and folklore, past and future and hold conversations that might just go somewhere.

Together these elements build a compelling truth which, in only five years, has spoken directly to the hearts and minds of millions of visitors. The rising of the Biomes in a post-industrial wasteland has become a persuasive metaphor for regenerative ingenuity – social as well as economic. Through them, their contents and the creativity they inspire we can better understand the challenges of the present as we seek a sustainable future for our children and the communities they will live in.

Education, arts and horticulture are joined by science and technology to help create the display. Creating Eden's exhibits and growing our plants requires a huge scientific input from a range of disciplines. The Science Team at Eden has three distinctive roles. The first is to undertake the research and application of principles needed to make the site work. Specific challenges have included the formulation of soil for establishing the Biomes. Starting from a china clay pit and associated spoil heaps

set the challenge of producing a substrate capable of growing a garden to showcase the world's plant diversity, using mine waste and organic wastes. Scientists work with our horticulturists to ensure that we display top-class living plant material from which the stories can be told. The second role is the development of background information, the research base that underpins many of our exhibits. Frequently it is impossible to demonstrate on site the full depth and complexity of this background work, although the exhibits are authentic representations down to the smallest detail. The garden adjacent to the Malaysian House in the Tropics Biome, for example, is based on surveys carried out by research students in the Danum Valley in Sabah, Malaysia, and is accurate down to the weeds that are planted amongst the crops. The Science Team also has a range of outreach projects and partnerships, many of which feed ideas and content into the displays –

for example, conservation work in the Seychelles and St Helena (see page 56).

We also run formal education programmes, for children and adults alike, and these similarly influence the exhibits and trails. Our innovative schools education programmes, attracting groups from all over the UK and beyond, link schools into real issues and current global stories. Look out for children chasing clues with the Crazy Chef and clambering through the rainforest on the Don't Forget Your Leech Socks programme. Again outreach also plays a role – the Gardens for Life project being an example (see page 104). Some of our exhibits are dedicated to showcasing their initiatives.

The Foundation and the Destination

The Eden Trust is the charity that owns and oversees the Eden Project. Eden Trust's charitable aims require it to run Eden as an education project, advancing the understanding of how we are dependent on natural resources, especially plant-based ones, and how we need to find ways of balancing our use of those resources with effective conservation. We talk of Eden as a stage, a place to show and celebrate the works of others, but of course we want to play our part as well, both by supporting positive change by others and through our own actions.

To do this, we established within Eden a team called the Foundation – a term we use to mean the underpinning of what we do. The team manages the educational work of Eden, as well as outreach and partnership projects in areas such as conservation and science. One thing we did not want to do, however, was to build a group divorced from the day-to-day operations of the Project, since these are one of the main ways that we can have a direct impact, especially locally. This size of the business is such that many skills are required for it to succeed. The Eden Project Destination runs all its services (catering, cleaning, retail) directly. People need to listen to and respect each other's competencies to make the place operate well.

Our catering and retail operations provide a means by which we implement our strong policy of sourcing locally and support producers of products that drive forward good environmental or social practice. Waste management challenges have allowed us to develop a new initiative, Waste Neutral (see page 172), around which we have built a major new public education programme including a waste compound open to visitors so that they can see how our rubbish is put to good ends. Our transport provides the chance to gain experience, and support the introduction, of environmentally friendlier fuels such as biodiesel. Our construction programme in particular, in conjunction with the wider Design and Construction Team, has provided an opportunity to develop buildings that embody and stretch the ideas of what good construction should look like. It is important for us to live by the standards we believe in, to walk the walk as well as talk the talk, but we need to go beyond that. Eden's charitable aims require that we develop a learning culture: one that experiments and innovates rather than implements current ideas of best practice. Our actions are local, but our thinking should go much further.

Recipe for Eden

1. Take an exhausted, deep, steep-sided clay pit.
2. Raise around £40 million to match the initial grant from the Millennium Commission.
3. Carve into a flat-bottomed bowl and landscape the sides.
4. Mix and add 83,000 tonnes of soil made from recycled waste.
5. Add superb architecture that draws inspiration from nature.
6. Colonize with a huge diversity of plants, many that we use every day (but don't often get to see).
7. Harvest the water draining into the pit and use it to irrigate our plants (and flush the loos!).
8. Season with people from all walks of life working in science, art, technology, education, commerce ...

Cook for a few years to create a beautiful site to celebrate our place in nature.

Eden is a work in progress: a symbol of the strength of people working with nature.
Degraded environments can be repaired.

It's amazing what you can do if you put your mind to it!

27

Biodiversity

Biodiversity is a rather nasty word that has tended to replace 'nature' in policy documents and scientific reports – perhaps because somehow it sounds more important. Biodiversity is simply life in all its richness and variety.

Nature is important because we are part of it, and it sustains us in innumerable ways. In many people's minds 'nature' means wild things, untamed things, but we should also remember that many of the common and domesticated creatures around us are just one step away from the wild. Not only is nature the source of all the natural products we use – foods, fuels, fibres, materials and medicines, to name but a few, and now even genes – but we are now beginning to learn lessons from nature as well as use it. The science of biomimicry promises enormous advances in making new materials (from Velcro based on weed seeds to self-ventilating T-shirts based on pine cones) and developing efficient systems with reduced waste (see page 172) by mimicking nature.

'To protect the environment costs a lot. To do nothing will cost much more.'   *Kofi Annan*

If you are not convinced about the importance of biodiversity, just think about your own body. Where does the individual called 'you' end? Your body is actually a partnership. You function because of a rich variety of other species that live on and in you – bacteria mostly, but other organisms are involved – keeping you alive. Take them away and you would collapse. Perhaps the most amazing fact is that our cells are believed to be a partnership between more primitive organisms that came together for mutual advantage. There is no such thing as an individual human – we are not one organism but ecosystems in our own right.

Of course the partnership does not end there: you are part of a much wider web of life. How wide no one really knows. We have 'seen and named' between one and two million species, but researchers estimate that the total number of organisms on Earth is anywhere between ten and one hundred million – the margin of ignorance is extraordinary. Of course most of these unknown species are pretty small – microbes, plants, fungi and invertebrates – but they are also the ones that do a lot of the work of keeping the Earth ticking over, cycling air, water and nutrients and trapping energy from the sun.

It is comforting in a way to recognize that life is remarkably adaptable. No matter how much havoc we cause, life on Earth will not end. It has survived amazing catastrophes and changes – meteoroid strikes, volcanic eruptions worse than any nuclear war and even a complete change of atmosphere from one with huge amounts of carbon dioxide to one with huge amounts of oxygen. However, human impact is causing many species to disappear and with them the

patterns of life, and the outputs on which our lives, and certainly our economies and societies, depend.

Richard Leakey, expert on human evolution and paleoanthropologist, believes that humans could trigger, even cause, the sixth extinction,

Living skyscrapers in the rainforests of Borneo

'*Most conservation effort goes into birds and mammals ... yet arguably it's the little things that run the world, things like soil microbes. They're the least-known species of all.*'

Lord May, President of the Royal Society

'The last word in ignorance is the man who says of an animal or plant: "What good is it?" ... If the biota [living world] in the course of aeons has built something that we like but do not understand, then who but a fool would discard seemingly useless parts? To keep every cog and wheel is the first precaution of intelligent tinkering.'
Aldo Leopold (1887–1948)

which would mean the loss of many species, possibly including our own. The *IUCN Species Survival Programme* agrees: 'The world's species face an unprecedented crisis. The rate at which they are being lost is alarming, even when compared with the [fifth] extinction episode of 70 million years ago when the dinosaurs disappeared. Recent calculations by leading scientists put it [the current extinction rate] at between 1,000 and 10,000 times greater than it would naturally be.'

In 2003 the World Conservation Monitoring Centre Red List showed that 12,000 species out of the 40,000 assessed, including 13 per cent of all flowering plants, faced extinction.

What is causing this crisis? In the last fifty years our numbers have doubled, leaving less room for other species. We are not managing our planet sustainably. Threats we are imposing that lead to loss of biodiversity include:

- habitat destruction
- climate change
- pollution
- disease
- urbanization
- agriculture
- over-harvesting of economically/culturally valuable wild plants
- spread of alien, invasive species knocking out the local species.

The list goes on. Most of these threats are not intentional. They are by-products of the way we live. The rich nations consume, making demands on the natural environment that cannot be met. The poor nations are forced to adopt lifestyles that also lead to the destruction of critical habitats.

Biodiversity loss is an issue to us because if it goes too far, despite the fact we are currently bucking the trend we will be among its first victims. An analogy sometimes used is that of a pilot who is flying along and notices that the rivets holding the wing together are falling out one by one. It's impossible to say with certainty how long you've got, but you know it can't carry on.

One reason that we tend to prefer the word 'nature' to 'biodiversity' is that it seems to allow more room for the less tangible benefits that other living things bring us – the poetry, the wonder, the inspiration. Even if major disaster is averted, every year too many beautiful things disappear, taking possibilities with them.

Finding a way to live on the Earth, and meet our needs, while sustaining the richness of other life is one of the most important challenges of the twenty-first century. Eden's single most important message to its visitors is to remind them of the myriad ways in which we depend on the natural world, every single second of every day, and to encourage people to reflect on what we need to do to sustain the world that sustains us. Some of our exhibits are *about* biodiversity – but every single one is actually a facet of biodiversity on display. Our entire site is a testament to the ability of nature to bring life back to degraded places, and a symbol that maybe one day we humans will learn how to leave the world better than we found it.

In this chapter we explore where biodiversity came from using examples from around the world and from conservation projects. We know we face challenges ahead, but one of Eden's roles is to show how people are rising to these challenges now.

In the beginning

The evolution of plant biodiversity, in fact all biodiversity, is a story of adaptation to changing terrestrial conditions. Today, plants clothe the world in a bewildering variety of shapes, sizes and colours and underpin the entire food web on land. To understand why we have such a huge array of plants we need to go back to the beginning, about 4,600 million years ago, to when the Earth was formed.

In the first 2,500 million years the planet changed from an inhospitable molten ball with no water or atmosphere to a place with continents, oceans, an almost breathable atmosphere and the first beginnings of life in the seas. The first living things were prokaryotes, microscopic single-celled bacteria-like organisms that probably evolved in hot deep-sea thermal vents about 3,500 million years ago. Some of these, cyanobacteria, were the first photosynthe-sizers, using the sun to turn carbon dioxide and water into sugar with oxygen as a by-product. This gas, vital to our survival, was poisonous to, and meant certain death for, many of the early life forms. Next came the multi-celled eukaryotes which had nuclei in their cells. This helped them to replicate, meaning that complex organisms could now evolve. Scientists believe that plants evolved when some of the primitive cells absorbed the green photosynthesizing cyano-bacteria, two creatures thus becoming one.

Next, 540 million years ago, worms and jellyfish evolved but plant life was still relatively simple. Life was limited to the seas, and algae, the dominant vegetation of the time, did not really have any reason to evolve much further, except at the margins of the sea where it met the land. (New things always seem to evolve on the edge.) Here the ancestors of mosses, liverworts and hornworts (bryophytes) began to develop. To make the move on to dry land, plants had to overcome some quite serious obstacles. Out of the water they had to survive alternate freezing and heating, drying out, the ravages of solar radiation and gravity. They also had a couple of really tricky problems: how to become self-supporting and how to drink. Eventually, some tiny bryophytes evolved an internal plumbing system which served two purposes: to transport water and to hold them up.

The first recognizable 'plant' to evolve on land was *Cooksonia*. About 6 centimetres tall, it had no leaves, flowers or seeds – just round stems and spore sacs. These vascular plants then started to grow bigger, gather more sunlight, take up water through roots and develop waterproof coatings and tiny holes in the leaves that allowed them to breathe. However, they still needed to be covered in a film of water to reproduce effectively. The history of the

evolution of plant life and its eventual dominance on land is a chronicle of sexual experimentation to overcome this single basic obstacle.

Ferns came up with one solution. Their fronds produced wind-dispersed spores which 'hatched' when they landed on damp ground into mini-paddling pools which produced eggs at one end and sperm at the other. The latter swam across to the egg and fertilized it. About 350 million years ago, the huge tree ferns, massive clubmosses and horsetails appeared, some of which eventually grew to 18 metres tall. It was the vast swampy forests of these plants, dying and falling into stagnant anaerobic water where they did not decay fully, that eventually formed coal deposits.

Around 290 million years ago, along came gymnosperms. These plants produced seeds and had worked out how to reproduce without water. These cycads, ginkgos, conifers and seed ferns became the dominant plants on land from about 250 million to 90 million years ago. Examples of these ancient species can be found on Eden's steep north-facing slopes.

Today flowering plants (angiosperms) have the upper hand. After a slow start they took the lead after dinosaurs became extinct. Their success was due to their reproductive strategy, which was to do it fast and produce variable offspring in case things changed. Angiosperms started to shape the world as we know it, and one sort in particular, the grasses, which came along 15 million years ago, really painted the landscapes. They affected the evolutionary trends of many animals, including a group of primates that walked on two legs rather than four, and who began to use their arms and hands for tool-making rather than climbing. Three of these grasses, maize, wheat and rice, went on to become the most dominant plant species on the planet (see page 80).

Biodiversity of plants

Currently there are an estimated 250,000 to 400,000 plant species on Earth, which have adapted, as we have, to live in a wide range of environments from the Arctic to the Equator. Like us, plants need to eat, drink, reproduce and protect themselves from danger. Unlike us, they can't walk about. They have evolved a wide range of strategies to move from place to place, which partly explain their diverse range of shape, colour and size.

From the humid tropic regions

In Eden's Humid Tropics Biome you can travel through the world's rainforests, including those of West Africa, Malaysia and South America in a single day. At first glance the plants in each region may look the same, but most of them are unique to their own geographical location. They look similar because they have all evolved and adapted to thrive in the humid, hot jungles of the world. This process is termed convergent evolution. Leaves tend to be big, shiny and fairly dark green: big to absorb the sun and to keep cool by transpiring (sweating out) water; shiny to help water to run off (aided by the guttering systems and drip tips often found on these leaves); and dark green to absorb more light in the overgrown darkness – only around 2 per cent of the light filtering through the rainforest trees reaches the forest floor. Some plant leaves here have evolved purple backings that reflect the sunlight back up through the leaf for a double dose. Plants such as begonias have white and silver lenses on their leaf surfaces to direct the light to the right place. Other species just make a break for the light, growing several metres a year to get their 'solar panels' into an advantageous position. Some have evolved as climbers in order to hitch a quick ride to the light, while others spend their whole lives high in living skyscrapers – the huge trees.

From the warm temperate regions

In Eden's Warm Temperate Biome, the Mediterranean, California and South Africa are represented. These areas, along with parts of Chile and Australia, fall within 30–40°N and 30–40°S of the Equator. The climate tends to be hot (up to 50°C) and dry in the long summers and wet and cool in the winters (temperatures rarely going below 0°C). The plants here have had to learn to defend themselves. To reduce water loss many leaves are small, thick and leathery. This is true in the Mediterranean – as in the case of French lavender (*Lavandula stoechas*);

Banana leaves have a gutter to remove excess water

in South Africa – tree heath (*Erica arborea*); and in California – Chamise (*Adenostoma fasciculatum*). Other plants develop hairs and are matt green, grey or even silver in colour to reflect the sun. Examples are the olive (*Olea europaea*), South African silver tree (*Leucadendron argenteum*) and the Californian lilacs (*Ceanothus* spp.). Tall, columnar shapes also decrease exposure to sunlight as, for example, with oleander (*Nerium oleander*) in the Mediterranean, restios (*Restios* spp.) in South Africa and manzanita species (*Arctostaphylos* spp.) in California. Since leaves are all-important solar panels many plants in these regions retain them year-round. Purple sage (*Salvia leucophylla*) grows lush larger leaves in the winter months and smaller leaves in the summer.

Plants here have also evolved to survive being eaten or burnt. Spines and aromatic oils keep off some herbivores, while other techniques protect them from destruction by licking flames – some plants send out new growth from the base of the stem after fire, while others produce seeds that will be dispersed and germinate only after the plants have come into contact with smoke or ash. These fast germinators are able to grow before the other plants arrive and compete for resources such as water. Bulbs, common in these regions, have adapted to the hot dry summers with a period of dormancy. Rather than compete for scarce resources they store energy below ground and grow and flower in the cooler autumn, winter and spring months. Snowdrops (*Galanthus* spp.) are a good Mediterranean example, gladiolus (*Gladiolus* spp.) are well known from South Africa and the Douglas' iris (*Iris douglasiana*) is an example from California.

The thin shape of restios protects them from harsh sunlight

Small, leathery leaves help reduce water loss

From the cool temperate regions

Familiarity may breed contempt but the plants on our own doorstep and further north also look and act as they do for good reason. Our deciduous trees make the most of our summers but shut up shop over winter. After the trees have reabsorbed the goodness from the leaves these spent solar panels fall to the ground. Conifers, originating further north, keep their dark-green needle-like leaves year round, making the most of any light that comes their way. Their conical shape means that snow slides off and doesn't break them. Plants that have taken up residence in high places, alpines, often look a little like their warm temperate relations – small spiky plants with small leaves. Why? Well, it may not be as hot and dry as it is in warm temperate areas but the wind dries out the leaves and the herbivores are just as hungry in cool temperate places.

From the dry tropic regions

As well as a quarter of the world's people, a wide range of extraordinary plant species live on the edge in the inhospitable, dry regions of the world, including deserts.

Many familiar cacti that grow in these regions are well supplied with spines, hooks and irritating hairs that keep them off the menu. Some, with none of these defences, use other tactics. As the first Americans found out thousands of years ago, some plants produce hallucinogenic compounds that limit their use for both humans and animals. Cacti are only found in the New World, the Americas. Euphorbias, which grow both in the Old World and the New, have adapted by quickly dropping their leaves when it gets hot. Like cacti they tend to be succulent and armed with spines. For their chemical armoury they have a milky sap that burns, as travellers lost in the desert and desperate for a drink have found to their cost.

A conifer's dark leaves soak up light all year round

Prickly cacti protect themselves from predators

Some insects and other animals use the defences of desert plants to their advantage. In the Kalahari Desert of Africa poisonous beetles get their toxins from milkweed (*Asclepias* spp.).

Many desert plants have thick, hard or resinous leaves that keep off predators and reduce desiccation by hot dry winds. The common gum cistus (*Cistus ladanifer*) on the edges of the Sahara Desert; the creosote bush (*Larrea tridentata*) in the Sonoran Desert of Arizona and California; the mesquites of the Sonoran and Chihuahuan Desert on the US/Mexican border; the acacia trees of the Kalahari Desert of Africa and the Simpson Desert of Australia – all have successfully evolved to cope with the extremes of heat and aridity. Mostly, they do so with a combination of two forms of root system – one that spreads widely just under the ground surface to catch any rain, and another that sends a tap root down to seek out any ground water.

Some plants have even evolved to live almost underground. Living stones (*Lithops* spp.) grow with only the tips of their stems above ground, and even these are covered by light-reflecting protective layers. Similarly there are cacti in the Atacama Desert in Chile that grow 90 per cent underground.

Flowers from all regions

You can often find the same-shaped flowers, such as butterfly-shaped members of the legume family (*Leguminosae*), in different climates. Flowers, the international beauties, are less tied to climatic zones as they are designed for reproduction. So why is there a huge variation between blooms in colour, shape and form? It's all a matter of breeding.

Some plants use spines for protection, others use milky sap

Bright, beautiful blooms attract pollen-spreading insects

Plants need a mechanism to transfer pollen from one plant to another in order to introduce variety into their offspring. Grasses and some trees have wind-pollinated flowers; these are not very showy, as they are not trying to attract attention, but they hang out to catch the wind. Many trees from temperate areas tend to flower and let their pollen drift in the breeze in the spring before the leaves appear and get in the way. But with plants for which animal go-betweens act as pollinators the flowers have evolved into a showy fashion parade with bright petals, scents and rewards of nectar and pollen for those attracted to the party.

The main go-betweens are insects. The plant and insect species that have been identified so far together represent two-thirds of all kinds of organism known to exist on this planet. Their joint leadership is no accident. Today there are whole complexes of mutually dependent plant and insect species which have evolved to rely on each other for their existence. Many people regard insects as a nuisance – some sting, some bite and some eat our vegetables and fruit – but without them many flowering plants could not reproduce.

Around 80 per cent of our food plants worldwide depend on pollinators and 30 per cent of our food and drink comes from seeds and fruits, all the result of flower fertilization. Since we are dependent on plants, we are also dependent on their associated biodiversity, including the insects and other pollinators which keep many of them going.

When Darwin was shown the beautiful Angraecum orchid (*Angraecum sesquipedale*) from Madagascar, he noted the 30-centimetre-long tube at the back of the flower with nectar at the bottom and predicted that a moth with a tongue at least 30 centimetres long would be needed to pollinate it. After Darwin's death, a moth was discovered in Madagascar with a tongue exactly 30 centimetres long. It was the pollinator and was named *Xanthopan morgani praedicta* (the last word because it had been formally predicted).

Long-tongued
Short-tongued
Snout-nosed
Bees,
Butterflies,
Beetles,
Hawkmoths ...
Dine on
Nectar à la carte,
Pollen fricassée,
Propolis flambé ...
From
Cuckoo pint,
Eyebright,
Meadow clary,
Apple blossom,
Periwinkle,
Fennel ....
Who are perfumed and dressed in
Purples,
Pinks,
Oranges,
Blues.

Annamaria Murphy

More than just a nut

The nuts of Bertholletia excelsa, *commonly known as Brazil nuts, grow in fist-sized pods containing up to twenty-five kernels. Trees can reach 150 metres in height and live for up to five hundred years. However, the plant's reproductive success depends mainly on the males of just one species of bee and two types of rodent with unusually strong, sharp teeth.*

The males of the long-tongued orchid bee are the only insects strong enough to open the coiled hood of the huge yellow flower of this tree, and have tongues that are long enough to reach the pollen and nectar. These bees visit tree after tree of this species, spreading the pollen, which leads to successful fertilization.

The nuts that then form have a very hard shell which hardly any creature can open. The agouti, a herbivorous rodent with extremely hard, sharp teeth, and a certain squirrel are the only animals able to strip off the husk of the nut. They store their food for lean months but often forget their caches, leaving the nuts to germinate and become saplings.

Because of this very specific and idiosyncratic method of symbiotic reproduction these trees are correspondingly difficult to cultivate. Therefore the annual crop of Brazil nuts collected each year (around 450,000 tonnes from the Brazilian Amazon forests alone) is usually taken directly from trees in the wild. If overcollected, this leaves few chances for natural replacement of the trees over time. Sustainable harvesting techniques are now being investigated to find a solution to this problem.

The palm family

The Palm exhibit in Eden's Humid Tropics Biome is devoted to showing palms' great diversity as a group. In most people's minds palms live in deserts or on the streets of Los Angeles, but in reality many also live in the humid tropics, both in the rainforest and as crops. They are as important to the economies of the tropics as cereal grasses are to temperate regions. They are also a very ancient group, at least sixty-five million years old.

There are about 2,800 species worldwide, most of them within the humid tropics and subtropics from 44°N to 44°S of the Equator. These species are distributed very unevenly: the New World has the lion's share at around 1,100 species, whereas continental Africa has hardly any, with the exception of Madagascar, which, like many islands, is rich in genera that have evolved there and there only. South-east Asia is very rich in palms, particularly the so-called 'understorey' species which love shade. Many palms have evolved in limited areas within continents and have become specialized; these are known as local endemics. The only palm to be genuinely pantropical in distribution is the coconut, whose seeds wash up on shores worldwide. Overall, it is thought that palms are on the decline – having been more widespread in the Eocene period (when species occurred along the Thames!) – because of cyclical cooling of the climate.

Next time you see a palm take a look at the leaves: they will look either like fans or like feathers. Eden's display shows a few modifica-

Brazilian wax palms

tions of this basic division – such as the undivided large leaves of species such as the handsome but unpronounceable *Johannesteijsmannia* or the well-named fishtail palms (*Caryota* spp.), which have pinnate leaves with fishtail-like leaflets.

The variety of growth types found in palms, including climbers, aquatics and palms that branch, is impressive. Climbing palms are known as 'rattans' and their stems, once their vicious spines have been removed, are an extremely useful forest-extractive material, particularly in South-east Asia, where they are used for making bentwood furniture. There are even a few species of aquatics: Nipah palm (*Nypa fruticans*) from South-east Asia, Aguaje palm (*Mauritia flexuosa*) from the Amazon and the Everglades palm (*Acoelorraphe wrightii*) from Florida. Branched palms, like *Hyphaene* spp., are in general limited to drier regions or deserts and will be species for our proposed Dry

Tropics Biome. The finest tree palms are in the arecoid botanical grouping and are noteworthy for their long, usually green, sheathing leaf bases which form a handsome 'crownshaft' at the top of the trunk and below the crown of leaves. These palms include the Royal palm (*Roystonea regia*), a key species for ornamental avenue planting, and the sealing wax palm (*Cyrtostachys renda*) with a bright red crownshaft. This palm lines the avenue into town from Singapore airport.

Though overwhelmingly a tropical family, palms occupy a very diverse set of habitats within these tropical regions. Some grow as emergents from the forest canopy, some in the understorey and others in communities in savannah lands. Some form clumps, whereas others are climbers. Different palm species live on limestone soils, in swamps, on mountains, in sand dunes or in the semi-desert. Occasionally, palms form monocultures in certain habitats.

Palm leaves come in all shapes and sizes

Coconuts wash up on beaches all around the world

Coconut palms in the Mafia Islands, Tanzania

For example, Nipah palm forms huge stands in South-east Asian swamps and coconuts (*Cocos nucifera*) form sizeable natural stands on Caribbean islands.

Only a handful of palms have become very important economically as plantation crops, used to make margarine, cattle food and many processed foods. The most important oil-producing plants of the tropics, fast-growing and yielding in three to five years, are the African and American oil palms, *Elaeis guineensis* and *E. oleifera* and hybrids between them. Vast areas of West Africa and South-east Asia, including much former rainforest, are laid to this palm. Coconut (*Cocos nucifera*) is planted for copra (its dried nut flesh, used in margarine, soap and cosmetics), milk, coir fibre and leaf thatch. Both of these plants have exhibits devoted to them at Eden.

Despite the fact that not many palms are grown as field crops, economic uses are diverse. Examples include sago from *Metroxylon sagu* (the tapioca of school dinners), 'hearts of palm'

Oil palm seeds after the harvest in south-west Cameroon

(the terminal bud from genera such as *Euterpe*, known as millionaire's salad because harvesting it kills the palm) and waxes for polish and lipstick from the Carnauba-wax palm (*Copernicia prunifera*). Everywhere palms are used as sources of thatching material, alcoholic saps of incredible potency (toddy, arrak or jaggery), matting, brooms, basketry, ropes, impromptu umbrellas and binding fibres (see also pages 196–7 for other uses). Some have significant cultural uses: the betel nut, *Areca catechu*, is sliced, mixed with lime and a leaf of the betel pepper (*Piper betle*) and chewed as a mildly narcotic 'quid' which stains the teeth red. The date (*Phoenix dactylifera*) is the oldest cultivated palm. Of vast importance to Arab nations, Arab cuisines and the survival of nomadic peoples, this is also grown as a plantation crop in arid regions.

In the tropics, palms are used to produce instant landscapes because they transplant well. In temperate regions they have had a great impact on glasshouse design. Because of their ancient lineage, generally slow growth, and requirements for both heat and height, growing them in specially designed 'palm houses' was the preserve of the wealthy (for example, the Duke of Devonshire for whom Joseph Paxton designed the Great Conservatory at Chatsworth) or of institutions looking to become more prestigious (such as the Royal Botanic Gardens, Kew, where the Palm House was designed by Richard Turner and Decimus Burton). Only in the Biomes at Eden, however, will tree palms be able to grow to their full height without being cut down before maturity as they are in glasshouses.

Despite their usefulness to humankind, palms, including many of the species shown at Eden and about half of the species in Kew's Palm House, are increasingly threatened by habitat loss caused by population pressure, logging and shifting cultivation. Some palms reach such iconic status that they have become protected in reserves by concerned governments. Usually palms can be propagated only by seed.

Biodiversity hotspots

There are some twenty-five areas of the world that have an unusually high diversity of species in any given area. These are known as 'biodiversity hotspots'. They are seen as important for conservation because protecting these areas has a big impact on slowing extinction.

Of course one of the reasons we need to protect biodiversity is that it provides services to us, such as clean air, water and soil. This means we need healthy plant and animal communities everywhere, not just in reserves and hotspots.

In the tropics

What they say about tropical plants is true: big plants engender big thinking. Tropical areas that are extremely diverse in all forms of biodiversity, including mammals, plants and insects, are aptly described as 'megadiversity countries'. On the list are Colombia, Ecuador, Peru, Brazil, Zaire, Madagascar, Malaysia, Indonesia and Australia. Some of these areas are represented in the Humid Tropics Biome at Eden.

Tropical South America is one of the richest and most diverse regions on Earth. It includes a strip on the west coast called the Tropical Andes that contains 15–17 per cent of the world's plant life in only 0.8 per cent of its area. This huge hotspot, 1,258,000 square kilometres in area, extends north–south from western Venezuela to northern Chile and Argentina and includes large portions of Colombia, Ecuador, Peru and Bolivia.

Victoria lily

45

The Humid Tropic Biome captures the magic of the tropical wet and moist forests that occur in tropical South America between 500 and 1,500 metres (the lowlands), and touches upon the cloud forests that extend from 800 to 3,500 metres. The montane cloud forests cover more than 500,000 square kilometres in Peru and Bolivia and are among the richest and most diverse forests on Earth.

Malaysia fits within an area called the Sundaland hotspot, which covers the western half of the Indo-Malayan archipelago, an arc of 17,000 Equatorial islands between the Asian mainland and Australia. Sundaland is bordered by the Wallacea, Indo-Burma and Philippines hotspots, and includes two of the largest islands in the world: Borneo and Sumatra. Most of Sundaland's 1.6 million square kilometres (75 per cent) falls within Indonesia, 21 per cent is in Malaysia; and the remaining 4 per cent falls within Singapore, Brunei and a small portion of southern Thailand. Tremendous variety exists between different levels in the hotspot's eco-sytems. Lowland rainforest is dominated by the towering rainforest giants known as *dipterocarps*. Sandy and rocky coastline harbours stands of beach forest, while muddy shores are lined with mangrove forests, replaced inland by large peat swamp forests.

While the whole of Sundaland was probably once covered with forest, today only 700,000 square kilometres of forest remain – less than half of the original area. This surviving area is highly fragmented, with only 125,000 square kilometres in more or less pristine condition. The most enduring pristine habitat lies in the interior of Borneo and within key protected areas in Sumatra and peninsular Malaysia.

Biologically, Sundaland is one of the richest hotspots on Earth, with about 25,000 species of vascular plants, 15,000 (60 per cent) of which are found nowhere else. One plant family, the *Scyphostegiaceae*, is confined to the hotspot and represented by a single tree species.

Tree diversity in Malaysia is spectacular. There are 3,000 species, including 267 from the family *Dipterocarpaceae*, the commercially

Tropical South America is one of the richest and most diverse regions on Earth

The Malaysian rainforest contains over 3,000 species of tree

47

valuable South-east Asia hardwoods. No fewer than 155 of these are endemic to the island. Endemic plants are confined naturally to a particular and usually very restricted geographic area or region. Malaysia also has more than 2,000 species of orchids. Sumatran forests include 105 dipterocarp species, 11 of which are endemic, and Java has 271 endemic orchids.

Notable plants in the hotspot include the members of the genus *Rafflesia*, sixteen species with very large flowers, one of which, *R. arnoldii*, has the largest flowers in the world at 1 metre in diameter.

West Africa includes two principal blocks of forest, which incorporate several important areas. The first block, Upper Guinea, stretches from southern Guinea into eastern Sierra Leone and through Liberia and Côte d'Ivoire into western Ghana. The second block extends along the coast from western Nigeria to the Sanaga River in south-western Cameroon. The two blocks are separated by the Dahomeny Gap in Togo and Benin, an area of savannah and highly degraded dry forest.

The West Africa hotspot is one of the most critically fragmented regions on the planet. Only 182,348 square kilometres (14.4 per cent of its original forest cover) remain. Much of this remaining forest is exploited for hunting or timber and does not represent intact habitat. Only 126,500 square kilometres (10 per cent of its original cover) are considered to contain pristine forests.

The West Africa hotspot is home to an estimated 9,000 vascular plant species, 25 per cent of which are endemic. The Tai National Park in Côte d'Ivoire, Mount Nimba on the Liberia and Guinea border, Cross River National Park in Nigeria and Mount Cameroon support high levels of plant diversity and house many endemic plants. The African oil palm (*Elaeis guineensis*), widely planted throughout the tropics for oil production, is native to this area. Timber extraction occurs nearly everywhere within the hotspot, including protected areas, the most valuable species being African ebony (*Diospyros gracilis*), two genera of African mahogany, *Entandophragma* and *Khaya*, and African teak (*Milicia excelsa*).

Côte d'Ivoire, West Africa

Man-made hotspots

We are all part of the environment and have a huge influence on it. Many of the world's great landscapes appear to be natural environments, but quite often they have been shaped by human intervention over many centuries, and the question of whether a place is truly wild can be difficult to answer.

The steppe once covered the vast plains of Europe, Central Asia and Russia. The extremely dry summers in these regions meant there was not enough moisture to support tree growth, and drought-tolerant grassland developed with an abundance of spring- and early- summer-flowering grasses and herbaceous perennials. These species flower while there is moisture in the soil and then during the summer months become parched and die back.

The exact origin of the steppe is not known, but it is thought that a long history of human management of the grassland through livestock grazing and controlled burning in early spring to prevent the encroachment of trees and weed influenced its development.

Until the Middle Ages people lived on and moved through the vast steppe from Mongolia to Hungary. Many of the wild ancestors of the founder crops in the Fertile Crescent (see page 100) such as wild wheat, barley, lentils and chickpeas originated from the moister fringes of woodland steppe. Today much of these vast plains have been ploughed up to grow cereal crops and only small fragments of true steppe survive.

Throughout central Europe many man-made secondary replacement grasslands have developed as a result of the clearance of the extensive and ancient oak forests that once covered the land. In Hungary these areas are known as *puszta*.

In the UK a similar vegetation type develops where thin soils are unable to hold water during our dry summer months. The best examples are in East Anglia on the Breckland sands and on shallow limestone soils of south-east England.

How good it was then to go out into quietness!
The steppe's boundless seascape flows to the sky
The feather grass sighs, ants rustle in it,
And the keening mosquito floats by ...
You cannot go over the road past the fence
Without trampling the universe.

Boris Pasternak

49

In early spring the Steppe exhibit at Eden comes alive as the whole slope is covered in the distinctive yellow flowers of the cowslip (*Primula veris*) and a scattering of the purple-flowered pasque flower (*Pulsatilla vulgaris*) before the grasses begin to grow taller and dominate. Later into the summer colourful blooms including pinks, sages, spurges, geraniums, origanums and asphodelines help to create a species-rich grass sward.

The prairie grasslands of mid-west North America originally covered 1 million square miles. They are thought to have resulted from the controlled burning of woodland by the American Indians to make travelling around and hunting of game such as buffalo a lot easier. After ten thousand years this management practice has resulted in a grassland expanse devoid of any trees but incredibly rich in wild flowers.

In the late nineteenth century the arrival of European settlers brought about the displacement of the Indians and the dramatic loss of virtually the entire prairie. As the industrialization of North America began the rich soils were ploughed up and exploited for growing agricultural crops. A few fragments of the original prairie have survived along railway tracks and in protected nature reserves. Ecologists have thus been able to reconstruct the original lost vegetation and are now able to improve upon surviving prairie in reserves and to re-create completely new areas by resowing and replanting. Many Americans view the prairie grasslands as a last remnant of the natural world.

The prairie is a hard place to scratch a living; the growing season is short and the weather is harsh and unpredictable. Many farmers give up. However, some of the locals, both white and native Americans, are looking to re-create 'buffalo commons', where the buffalo can roam free once more. This initiative could help to regenerate the prairies and provide a means of

making a living through buffalo meat and tourism.

The semi-natural prairie ecosystem characteristically has tall wavy grasses with a profusion of mid- to late-summer-flowering herbaceous perennials. Repeated fires and grazing by livestock are necessary to maintain its existence and to prevent the encroachment of trees. In Eden's Prairie exhibit you will see the yellows of sunflower (*Helianthus* spp.), coneflower (*Rudbeckia*) and golden rod (*Solidago canadensis*) and the less well-known *Silphium* and *Ratibida* spp.. The tallest of all is the prairie dock (*Silphium terebinthinaceum*) that emerges from the typically metre-high vegetation to flower at 2.5 metres. Other colours are also present but less dominant, as in the pale blue flower of the prairie aster (*Symphyotrichum turbinellum*) and the purple of *Liatris aspera*. One of the first perennials to flower in mid-July is the distinctive echinacea (*Echinacea purpurea*), the roots of which contain chemicals that are known to stimulate the immune system and so help our bodies to fight off infections. Echinacea has been used traditionally by the Indians and is also a stunning ornamental garden plant.

Prairie-type planting using herbaceous perennials in a naturalistic way has recently become popular among landscape architects and designers. This radical way of creating a cost-effective yet beautiful display with low-maintenance requirements has great potential for the improvement of large urban green spaces where funding is often limited. Pioneering research in this area is being done by Dr James Hitchmough at the University of Sheffield landscape department.

The Mediterranean Basin is cool and wet in winter, and hot and dry in summer – a seasonal pattern that seems to promote diversity in plant species. Collectively and individually the regions with this climate contain thousands of different organisms, being particularly rich in small sub-shrubs and flowering bulbs.

The Mediterranean Basin is also one of the crucibles of human development. With the great civilizations of Egypt, Greece, Rome and Islam all having their roots in the region, it is not surprising that significant food crops, and even more significant farming technologies, have originated there.

To talk of harmony between farmers and the landscape may be naïve: the vast history of human exploitation of the land inevitably transformed the environment and favoured some species more than others. However, over thousands of years it produced a system that reached a balance, with many species and much

The Western Mediterranean climate is ideal for cork oaks

of the diversity dependent on the patchwork of cultivated and semi-natural land. Natural disturbances, such as fire, were adapted and used by early farmers to produce a form of shifting cultivation that was within the tolerance of many of the plants and animals that lived there.

The diversity survived over much of the Mediterranean until well into the twentieth century – as late as the 1970s farming techniques in southern Spain were almost unchanged from those of medieval times. The transformation since then has been one of the most rapid and significant shifts in European land use in recent history. One problem has been burgeoning urban development, which has had a particularly dramatic effect on lowland coastal strips, but the change in agriculture has been even more profound. Crops such as olives, traditionally produced in terraces, and mixed farming systems with plenty of room for wildlife, have been transformed by agribusiness production systems into plantations as intensive and sterile as any in the world.

Abandonment of the land can be just as threatening. The traditional *dehesas* or *montados* (cork production forests), in Spain and Portugal respectively, are regarded as some of the most biodiverse and sustainable farming systems in the world, particularly renowned for their bird populations. A loss of market to screwtops or plastic corks threatens their existence.

Eden's Mediterranean display therefore is dominated by Tim Shaw's dramatic Dionysus sculpture, representing a god who started out as the embodiment of law-giving, order and agriculture, and became the god of drunkenness and over-indulgence – a metaphor for local agriculture, which dances a fine line between supporting and threatening the biodiversity of the land.

Conservation solutions to the challenge of protecting the land are complicated, as they are across much of Europe, by the desirability of maintaining the patterns of disturbance, grazing and burning, typical of traditional agriculture, to which the plants and animal communities have adapted. Some countries, such as Spain, have protected impressively large areas of land by designating them National Parks, but the real answer to conservation may lie in changes to the Common Agricultural Policy of the European Union to encourage forms of production that sustain biodiversity rather than maximize yield at all cost.

Dionysus surveys his kingdom

52

Conserving biodiversity

Forest canopies

One of the steps in biodiversity conservation is to work out what's there and why it's important. Many of the important scientific questions relating to understanding tropical (and temperate) forests and the practical problems in managing these ecosystems require an understanding of the least-known layers, the forest canopy. Over the last thirty years a number of biologists have literally taken to the trees and become canopy specialists in order to address widespread and far-reaching issues such as extinction, water use, climate change and biodiversity.

The forest canopy is defined as the aggregate of all crowns in a forest stand. It plays a crucial role in the maintenance of biodiversity and the provision of local and global ecosystem services. Forest canopies support approximately 40 per cent of currently living species and also influence the hydrology of more than 45 million hectares of land by controlling evaporation and transpiration and intercepting up to 25 per cent of precipitation. Their removal often decreases local rainfall substantially. Remarkably, work at this challenging frontier only began in earnest in the early 1980s, and has already changed substantially our understanding of key ecosystem processes.

Forest canopies are among the most species-rich yet most highly threatened terrestrial habitats. Twenty-two of the twenty-five global biodiversity hotspots embrace forest habitat that combines high levels of endemism (indigenous species) with the imminent threat of degradation. Knowing the number of species is fundamental to formulating questions about ecosystem function and evolution, as well as informing conservation priorities.

A relatively high proportion of invertebrates – about 20 to 25 per cent – are proposed to be unique to the forest canopy. Ten per cent of all vascular plant species are canopy dwellers, living in the treetops and deriving their moisture and nutrients from the air and rain.

The montane cloud forests of Peru

How much? How fast?

'It is estimated that 1 per cent of rainforests (areas the size of England and Wales) are being cut down every year ... this means a high level of extinction as the wildlife which depends on the forest dies with it. This is caused by many factors, including:

- cattle ranching
- logging
- agriculture
- mining
- oil exploration and pipelines
- dam building.'

Rainforest Concern

The forest canopy is the interface between the atmosphere and 90 per cent of the life on Earth. Multidisciplinary research in the canopy has led to a greater understanding of the richness and importance of our global biodiversity, how our planet works and how forests and other ecosystems provide services such as cleaning our air and regulating our climate (see page 159). Changing the area of rainforest may greatly influence our climate; conversely climate change could greatly influence the biodiversity of the rainforest and the way the forests regulate our climate.

Forest conservation projects

Non-timber forest products (NTFPs) are commercial products, other than timber, that can be extracted from forests. Typical NTFPs include resins, oils and gums, medicinal plants, spices, honey, fruits and nuts (chestnuts, pine kernels, etc.). During the early 1990s NTFPs were considered to be a good way of enabling local people to farm forests without destroying them.

It's more complex than that. Recent research shows that more biodiverse-rich forested areas, considered to have greater conservation need, are

Relentless logging threatens rainforests across the globe

characterized by fewer individuals of specific species, which doesn't make them ideal for commercial harvesting. Forests with less biodiversity and clusters of the same type of plant are most conducive to commercial extraction.

NTFPs are important to the people who live in and off the forest. There is a global move towards devolving management of resources to local communities.

Fragile island floras

Islands, especially isolated ones, are true lost worlds, which often contain plants found nowhere else on Earth. They tend to have fewer species per unit area than the mainland. However, what they lack in number they make up for in unique plant life forms (endemics).

Sometimes these plants represent relics of a past age, sometimes they have evolved in isolation. A common phenomenon on islands is gigantism, where species or parts of a plant grow to extreme size. For example the coco-de-mer (*Lodoicea maldivica*), a type of palm found only on the Seychelles, has the largest seed in the world. Unlike coconuts, the seeds die in salt water; and they have also been over-harvested, both as trophies and for their perceived aphrodisiac qualities – they are shaped like a huge bottom. Nowadays every coco-de-mer seed in the Seychelles is registered and numbered.

The majority of recorded extinctions occurred on islands, making the study of evolution and conservation practice on islands a priority. Their ecosystems are under threat from introduced plants, pests and diseases, over-collection and habitat destruction, and a substantial proportion of our currently threatened species live on them today. Island populations therefore carry a global responsibility for the protection of biodiversity. Unfortunately these same populations are often extremely vulnerable to change and degradation, and available resources can be extremely limited. To match their global responsibility they need global support.

Worldwide conservation projects

'What we do with respect to small islands has implications far beyond their troubled shores. By working with small islands on their problems, we can find solutions for ours. Brighter horizons for small islands can mean brighter horizons for the world in general.'　　Kofi Annan

St Helena Working with the Weston Foundation, Eden supports a number of Ph.D. projects, including conservation projects in the Seychelles and St Helena. Famed as the prison and last home of Napoleon, St Helena is one of the most remote islands in the world, almost 2,000 kilometres from the west coast of Africa and nearly 3,000 kilometres from South America. In the early sixteenth century it was used as a staging post by the Portuguese, and goats were introduced to provide meat. Nearly 150 years later the island was settled under the East India Company. The goats' 'work' was then complemented by tree clearance, driving many of the island's plants towards extinction. The island paid the price: one-third became desert, prone to serious soil erosion. In 1834 it came under British rule. Today there is a population of 5,000 on the island, which has an area of a mere 122 square kilometres.

St Helena currently has forty-five surviving endemics, many of which have been pulled back from the edge of extinction. In 1998, for example, a boxwood (*Mellissia begoniifolia*) believed to be extinct was found and seed rescued before the parent plant died. At Eden some of the St Helena endemics feature in our Tropical Island display. They will be no more than living fossils until their island habitat can be restored for them. The conservation team on St Helena is working hard to reverse the processes of degradation and also re-establish endemic plants against a backdrop of introduced exotic plants. Until recently only a fragment of native gumwood forest remained on the island – fewer than 1,000 individuals. In an excellent example of public participation in conservation work the islanders marked the Millennium by planting 4,000 gumwood trees on degraded wasteland.

The Seychelles The Eden Project is working with the Seychelles to tell the story of conserving the land and native plant species in these fragile environments.

The Seychelles are a continental island group located in the Indian Ocean. They are unique in being considered part of the original Gondwanaland. The once-abundant native flora of the Seychelles is now sadly confined to just a few remaining small pockets.

It's not all doom and gloom, however. A collaborative effort with the Seychelles Ministry of the Environment, St Helena National Trust, University of Reading, Darwin Initiative and

Impatiens gordonii from the Seychelles

other supporters has already led to the completion of propagation, nursery and establishment protocols for 90 per cent of the Seychelles' endemic plants. To complement this, a Ph.D. project is under way to develop a species recovery plan for balsamine sauvage (*Impatiens gordonii*), an endemic plant of the Seychelles mist forests. There are only two known wild populations left in the world, consisting of around one hundred and twenty plants in total. A cultivar called *Impatiens* 'Ray of Hope' resulted from attempts to address genetic questions raised in this study. This plant is being sold through Eden, with permission from the Seychelles government, to raise awareness and the sales help to fund conservation of Seychelles endemic plants.

South Africa The Cape Floral Kingdom has one of the greatest varieties of plants on Earth; it is botanically richer than the rainforest. Fynbos, with around 7,000 plant species (5,000 of which occur nowhere else in the world), covers 80 per cent of this area, stretching for 70,000 square kilometres either side of the Cape, in a band no more than 200 kilometres from the southern coast. '*Fain-boss*' is Afrikaans for 'fine bush', which refers to the evergreen, fire-prone shrubs that live in the nutrient-poor soil.

The main plant groups are restios (rush-like plants), proteas (including the beautiful bird-like *Leucospermum* and *Leucadendron*), ericaceous plants and stunning lilies, orchids and irises.

Despite being able to survive fire, drought and poor soil, fynbos is one of the Earth's most threatened habitats. Nearly one-third of the original fynbos has been lost to burgeoning urban settlements, pollution, agricultural conversion and invasive alien tree species. More than 1,400 species are listed as being critically rare, endangered or vulnerable and at least twenty-nine have already become extinct. Land purchase and protection are essential to safeguard the plants and their habitat's future.

The fynbos of South Africa in all its glory

57

In 1999, Fauna and Flora International, the world's oldest international conservation body, used some of its emergency land purchase funds to buy Flower Valley, at the southernmost tip of Africa. The purchase saved 550 hectares of fynbos from being ploughed up to plant vines. The land is conserved but still produces a sustainable harvest – of cut flowers, from proteas to window-box geraniums and sweet-scented freesias, which are sold to the European market. Local people are also making 'fynbos paper' to provide a year-round income. Fauna and Flora International has also established sustainable harvesting methods on the farms surrounding Flower Valley, thus influencing the management and conservation of fynbos over 25,000 hectares.

In Flower Valley surplus income is re-invested in alien species clearance, the purchase of harvested wild flowers from local landowners and farmers, and the development of marketing plans and support for micro-enterprise activities based on fynbos products. The South African National Parks (SANP) are using Flower Valley as a model to support fynbos conservation.

In Flower Valley wages have increased, houses have been improved and an early learning centre and adult education facility opened. The people are seeing the richly diverse fynbos of Flower Valley and the surrounding countryside as a valuable resource that needs to be preserved for future generations. The South African government is using it as a model for its poverty relief programme.

Also in South Africa is Green Futures, a unique project linking conservation, horticulture and education. It serves the growing need for trained and knowledgeable staff to work in conservation-related horticulture and tourism in the region and directly supports some of the poorest communities. The training team is headed by Sean Privett, one of the leading conservationists in the Cape, who worked in the Warm Temperate Biome at Eden helping to refine and develop our South Africa displays. Also on the team is Hilary Bosher, one of the first graduates from Eden's own horticultural diploma.

Proteas and other exotics of South Africa

58

The Mediterranean Cork is the bark of the evergreen oak tree (*Quercus suber*). The Egyptians used cork for fishing floats 4,500 years ago, but today two-thirds of cork production is for stoppers. Fifteen billion corks are pulled from wine bottles every year. By-products of the industry are also environmentally friendly – flooring tiles, table mats, insulation, shoes and linoleum. There is even a layer of cork in the space shuttle.

Cork is durable, light, bouncy, chemically inert, impermeable and an excellent insulator. In the 1660s, Robert Hook looked down his newly invented microscope to discover why. Cork is made of millions of tiny prisms like a honeycomb. He called these 'cells'. A cubic centimetre of cork has 140 million cells, each half-full of gas to give cork its unique flexibility and compressibility. To harvest cork, there is no need to fell the tree because the bark is renewable. When the tree is around twenty-five years old, the bark is stripped for the first time – and then again every nine years. Only the third stripping produces bark good enough for corks, but a single tree can supply 3,000 corks at one strip and live for around two hundred years.

Cork oak forests are adapted to warm temperate/semi-desert climates. They form one of the few traditional, sustainable, rural economies to survive in Europe. They contain a greater diversity of plants and animals than any other commercial crop. Managed by thinning and pruning and the grazing of sheep, goats and the black Iberian pig, they need neither fertilizers nor pesticides. In some Portuguese villages 80 per cent of the inhabitants depend on cork forests. They produce luxury traditional foods such as specialist ham from the Iberian pigs and also honey, cheese and charcoal.

This traditional agro-forestry supports a remarkable abundance and variety of rare wildlife: the Iberian lynx (*Lynx pardinus*), probably the world's most endangered big cat; the Spanish imperial eagle (*Aquila adalberti*), the black vulture (*Coragyps atratus*), the booted eagle (*Hieraaetus pennatus*), Bonelli's eagle

Harvesting cork in Portugal

(*Hieraaetus fasciatus*) and the short-toed eagle (*Circaetus gallicus*), which makes giant nests in cork trees and eats snakes. Europe's entire population of cranes winters in the cork oak forests.

We can influence the conservation of the biodiversity supported by the cork oak forests. Currently 8 per cent of wine stoppers are synthetic or screwtop. If this proportion increases, cork forests are in trouble, because 90 per cent of exported cork is used for wine. You will never impress anybody by smelling a plastic stopper. But pull a real cork and you can say you are helping to save the Iberian lynx and forty-two species of birds. Another option is diversification. One fashion company in Europe is beginning to make extraordinary clothes, shoes and bags from cork that look like suede.

Cork transported the traditional way in Andalucia, Spain

Heather Jansch's cork pigs in the Warm Temperate Biome

Biodiversity on our doorstep

Although there are many hotspots in far-flung lands, we have a huge responsibility on our very own doorstep. Wild plants in the UK are under pressure; the worst hit counties are losing more than one plant every year. In the last fifty years we have lost: 98 per cent of wild flower meadows; 75 per cent of open heaths; 96 per cent of peat bogs; and 190,000 miles of hedgerow.

The main threats facing our wild plants include: intensive agriculture, inappropriate development (such as road building), neglect and mismanagement, peat extraction, illegal plant collection, pollution of soil and water, the spread of non-native invasive plants and the use of non-native plant varieties in landscaping and restorations.

Showcasing Cornish conservation projects

Cornwall has many varied habitats: Atlantic woodland, Cornish heathland, pastureland, field margins, Cornish hedges – all of which have been shaped by people. We have re-created these habitats at Eden in our Biodiversity and Cornwall exhibit. Why, if you can see the plants just down the road? Because, as Senegalese poet Barh Dioum says:

'In the end we will conserve only what we love. We will love what we know.'

To reconnect people with their own environments at Eden we use art, sculpture, poetry and prose to bring the landscapes to life.

Atlantic woodlands on the south-west coast of Cornwall are among the least disturbed of our semi-natural habitats. They contain native oak, willow, ash and hazel, pruned by the wind, dwarfed by the poor soil, and, thanks to the clean air, clothed in ferns, mosses and lichens.

These temperate rainforests have a rich diversity, but many species in them are often small, green and easily overlooked. English Nature is re-creating 500 to 1,000 hectares of woodland landscape in the Cornish clay area near Eden, restoring a habitat that would have been there until the last hundred years or so.

At Eden we are creating our own little piece of Atlantic woodland. Artist Kate Munro has worked with Eden's Green Team to create 'wind-pruned' metal trees, so typical of Cornish uplands. The real plants will take a little longer.

61

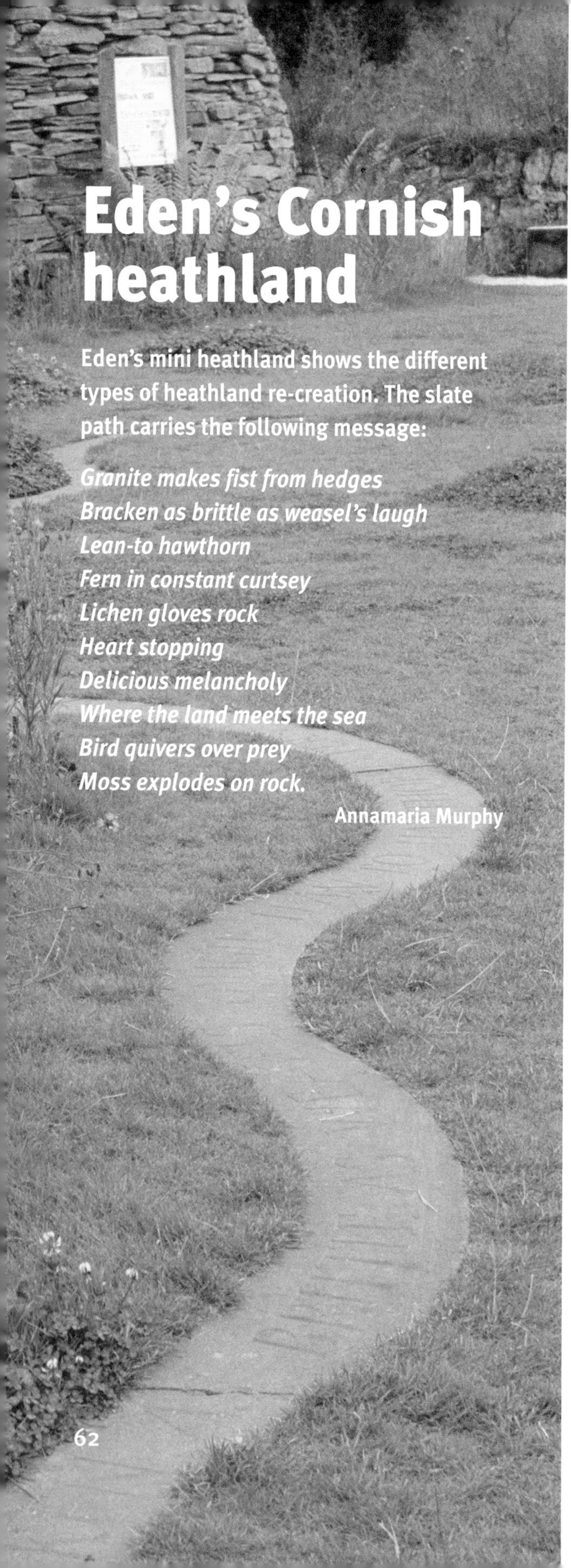

Eden's Cornish heathland

Eden's mini heathland shows the different types of heathland re-creation. The slate path carries the following message:

Granite makes fist from hedges
Bracken as brittle as weasel's laugh
Lean-to hawthorn
Fern in constant curtsey
Lichen gloves rock
Heart stopping
Delicious melancholy
Where the land meets the sea
Bird quivers over prey
Moss explodes on rock.

Annamaria Murphy

What am I?

Blood stopper
Heart catcher
The Devil's Buttonhole
I am the ruby
Of the hedges
Beloved of lovers' posies
Cock Robin
Lightning frightener.

Red campion
(*Silene dioica*)

Early gentian

Lowland Cornish heathland is rarer than
rainforest. We lose 15 per cent of it every ten
years, mostly because of non-management,
but this is now changing. Eden is working
with English Nature to show how heathland is
re-created, by:

- hydro seeding: seeds are sprayed on in a
  liquid carrier
- hand seeding and spreading of salvaged
  cuttings
- re-spreading of heathland soil and litter
  collected from existing heathland.

Once the heathlands provided sustenance –
fodder for animals and fuel for fires. Today they
provide recreation – and perhaps free-range meat
and heather beer. Eden's lowland heath was re-
created with the help of English Nature using
heathland topsoil, seeds and turfs from an
existing heath which was being moved as part
of a conservation project.

Endangered species in Cornwall Cornwall
and the Isles of Scilly are home to several rare
and endangered plants.

Some of Cornwall's rarities include:

- Early gentian (*Gentianella anglica*): one of
  the forty-five endemic plants known in
  Britain and Ireland. It is nationally scarce
  and part of Plantlife International's Back
  from the Brink species recovery programme.
- Babington's leek (*Allium ampeloprasum* var.
  babingtonii): nationally scarce, this plant,
  which can reach 1.5 metres tall, is now
  abundant on the Isles of Scilly.
- Small tree mallow (*Lavatera cretica*):
  considered extinct in Cornwall, but common
  on the Isles of Scilly, the small tree mallow
  can withstand the full scythe of Atlantic gales
  and spray. The last site in Cornwall, near
  Penzance, was destroyed by coastal flood
  defence work.

What can we do to save plants that are
endangered?

First, to save plants we need to save their
homes. English Nature and Plantlife International are helping to restore and re-create
habitats for endangered plants. The Cornwall
Heathland Project (see page 65) is a direct
result of the Cornwall Biodiversity Initiative, a
programme that sets priorities and reminds us
of our local responsibilities.

Interpreting endangered species in stone at Eden

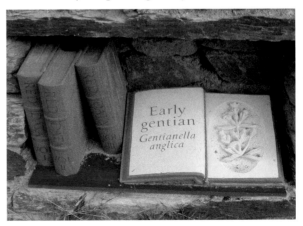

Stories of wild Cornwall

Three-quarters of the land in Cornwall is farmland, which in the right circumstances – unsprayed field margins, for instance – can provide rich habitats for beautiful (and useful) wild flowers. Cornish hedges, mini-mountains of soil and rock, are at once shady and sunny, dry and moist, providing a wide range of habitats for hundreds of plants and animals including dormice, toads, slow worms, beetles and thousands of other invertebrates.

Angie Bromley, one of Eden's guides, has developed a special relationship with the Wild Cornwall exhibit. She brings the exhibit alive with stories of the people who used to live off the land:

'A pretty native flower of springtime, the primrose (Primula vulgaris) loves to grow in hedgerows and byways. The leaves were once pounded into a sticky green salve to relieve the pain of aching or rheumatic joints. The leaves of common sorrel (Rumex acetosa) are quite acid, but a useful condiment when added to a broth, stew or casserole; and on the laundry days of yesteryear the juice of sorrel stems was often used to help remove ink or iron stains from linen or fine lace. Common heather (Calluna vulgaris), which loves the acid soils of Cornwall, was made into brushes or brooms to sweep earthen or slate floors. Soft rushes (Juncus effusus) were cut, and the outer layer of each stem stripped to expose a soft, spongy white pith. The long pith was then dipped either into melted beeswax or animal lard, dried and then used as a light for dark winter evenings.'

Supporters of Eden's Biodiversity and Cornwall exhibit

English Nature is the government agency for conservation and natural features in England. The Cornwall team is noted for its innovative landscape-scale ecological restoration projects in the Claylands. The Cornwall Heathland Project (Oberenn Rosvro Kernow in Cornish), a partnership project between English Nature, china clay companies IMERYS and Goonvean, and Cornwall County Council, is re-creating over 750 hectares of heathland in mid-Cornwall, much of which is on china clay waste tips. By 2007 the project, part of the Heritage Lottery Funded Tomorrow's Heathland Heritage programme, will have restored or re-created lowland heathland over an area the size of the Isle of Wight.

The Cornwall Biodiversity Initiative is a partnership of over a hundred organizations and individuals in Cornwall dedicated to conserving and restoring threatened habitats and species in the county.

Plantlife International is a charity dedicated exclusively to conserving all forms of plant life in the UK, Europe and across the world, in their natural habitat. Its Back from the Brink programme aims to reverse the declines suffered by threatened wild plants. Its Making it Count for People and Plants programme asks for help to survey common wild flowers around the country to provide an annual check and help to conserve them and their habitats. Eden worked with Plantlife on its County Flowers project, designed to celebrate and raise awareness of our native flora, by asking visitors to vote for their favourite county flower. Cornwall's winner was Cornish heath.

Global conservation strategies

We do not have a complete inventory of the plants of the world, but it is estimated that there may be anything between 250,000 and 400,000 species. As we have seen, many are in danger of extinction (see page 32), and halting the destruction of the plant diversity that is so essential to meet the present and future needs of humankind is one of the greatest challenges for the world community.

At the Hague in April 2002, a Global Strategy for Plant Conservation was endorsed, the long-term objective of which is to halt the continuing loss of plant diversity. Sixteen global targets for plant conservation were set, to be completed by the global community by 2010. The UK is committed to implementing the strategy, and its response – the first by any nation – is Plant Diversity Challenge, a partnership between the Joint Nature Conservation Committee, Plantlife International and the Royal Botanic Gardens, Kew, working on behalf of the government. In February 2004, Elliot Morley MP presented the Plant Diversity Challenge Report. It was launched at the Seventh Conference of the Parties to the Convention on Biological Diversity in Kuala Lumpur, Malaysia.

One of Eden's aims is to engage the public with issues surrounding biodiversity conservation and to show them ways in which they can get involved, putting them in touch with organizations through which they can play an active role. Working with Botanic Gardens Conservation International, Eden helped to compile Target 14 for the Global Strategy for Plant Conservation, which established 'The importance of plant diversity and the need for its conservation [to be] incorporated into communication, educational and public awareness programmes'. Effective education can inspire optimism, empowerment, motivation and action, and is therefore vital to the success of the global strategy. Not everyone is interested in issues relating to biodiversity conservation, however, so it's a matter of finding ways of connecting the subject to their everyday lives and/or inspiring interest in other ways. Many of the examples described in the Target 14 paper came from our experiences at the Eden Project.

Taru Brazil, an environmental education group, working at Eden

Conserving our cultivated plants

Of all the Earth's plant species, around 100,000 may be edible. About 7,000 are used in food and agriculture but only about thirty supply around 90 per cent of the world's calorie intake (and three of these – wheat, rice and maize – supply 68 per cent). Thanks to genetic diversity, environmental pressure and human selection food crops have evolved into a range of different forms consisting of thousands of cultivated varieties (cultivars). The species *Brassica oleracea*, for example, exists in many diverse forms, including crinkly Savoy cabbage, red cabbage, white cabbage, spring cabbage, cauliflower, calabrese, Brussels sprouts, kale – take your pick. What we see in the shops merely scratches the surface of crop diversity worldwide, ranging from modern hybrids to traditional landraces, varieties selected over millennia by farmers to suit their particular growing conditions and tastes. Farmers, particularly subsistence farmers with low income, have always grown a wide range of species and varieties as an insurance policy against crop failure. Farmers also traditionally favour diversity for taste and cultural reasons. Over time farmers replace poor performers with more desirable forms, often deliberately allowing varieties to cross and thus creating new varieties.

The conservation of crop biodiversity is vital for our survival. Over the past hundred years crop diversity has been eroded by increasing standardization of products linked to industrialization and increasing globalization, and the use of fewer modern high-yielding varieties. The number of potato varieties in the small island of Chiloe, off the coast of Chile, a once-important source of germplasm for global potato breeding, dropped from 200 varieties in the 1920s to 40 only fifty years later. Many landraces such as these, which have played an important role in the breeding of modern improved varieties, have now fallen out of favour for food production.

Landraces developed by farmers have important traits in terms of yield, taste, pest and disease resistance and adaptation to climate change – and are continuing to evolve. Their conservation is vital to future food security and for the welfare of farmers who wish to grow them.

Wild relatives are as important as landraces and cultivars. Wild sunflower species have been of great value for cultivated sunflower crop varieties. Most disease-resistance genes have come from the wild relatives. The estimated value of the wild species is as high as US $400 million annually. *Lycopersicon cheesmaniae,* a species of tomato from the coast of the Galapagos, has been used to breed salt resistance into commer-

Marigolds grown for commercial use in Los Mochis, Mexico

68

cial tomato varieties. Three wild peanuts have played a significant role in breeding for resistance to nematode, which costs industry around the world US $100 million a year.

Processes of conservation

Crop biodiversity can be maintained *in situ* on farmers' fields or community land or *ex situ* in genetic resource centres (gene banks). There is increasing interest in *in situ* conservation. Scientists have been working with farmers to maintain local diverse farming systems. Other initiatives include participatory plant breeding, where farmers work alongside scientists to maintain diversity and improve yields of traditional crops by crossing higher-yielding improved varieties with highly prized local landraces.

NGOs, in concert with local farmers, encourage the best 'seed savers' by organizing biodiversity fairs, where plant material and information can be exchanged and prizes offered for diversity. Women play an important traditional role in the conservation of crop biodiversity. In the Andes women sort potatoes by variety and size. The biggest tubers are kept for food, medium ones are saved as seed and small tubers are dried. In Mexico, Guatemala and southern China women play a role in selecting maize seeds for future cultivation.

Crop collections started before the nineteenth century, but the twentieth century witnessed a huge expansion in genetic resource centres. There are now some 1,470 around the world. These range in size from national to regional to the large global genetic resource 'Alliance of Future Harvest Centres' supported by the Consultative Group on International Agricultural Research (CGIAR). The centres carry out research, collect plant material, keep extensive records, safely store seeds to maintain their viability and hold much of their material in trust for humanity.

Not all plants can be stored as seeds. Apples have to be maintained in field genetic

Sorting potatoes in the Andes

resource centres as grafted trees. Bananas, which don't often have seeds, are conserved as very small plantlets in tissue culture medium. Some genetic resource centres now use liquid nitrogen that enables long-term storage of plant tissue without damage. Micro-propagation from tiny pieces of plant tissue enables the production of fresh virus-tested planting material that can be transported conveniently all around the world.

Genetic resource centres are the long-term reservoirs of biodiversity, an 'insurance policy' for future food needs. Scientists have already identified the need to double crop yields in the next fifty years just to keep pace with growth in human population levels. Governments often react to emerging crises with aid or support. By contrast longer-term social and scientific development often gets less media attention but

may be more effective at reducing the risk of poverty and instability and improving food security.

Unfortunately, funding for genetic resource centres has remained the same or been reduced in recent years. The scale of the problem is more severe in the developing world, which accounts for 80 per cent of the world's population, 80 per cent of the world's biodiversity, around 5 per cent of the world's scientists (if China, India, Brazil and Mexico are excluded) and only 15 per cent of the world's economy. A report prepared by the Department of Agricultural Sciences, Imperial College London, Wye Campus, and the international agricultural research community has highlighted the need for the establishment of a permanent endowment to ensure long-term funding.

Mixtures versus monoculture

The movement to a monoculture cropping system (growing a single species, often genetically very uniform) accelerated with industrialization and its greater emphasis on larger markets, economies of scale and increased uniformity. Risk of pests and diseases increased; the spread of potato blight in Ireland in the 1840s was made worse by growing susceptible potatoes derived from a narrow gene pool. Southern corn blight devastated maize varieties in the USA because all were susceptible to the disease, sharing as they did the same gene that had been used in breeding hybrid maize.

Asian soybean rust has been spreading around the world since its discovery in Japan in 1904. In 2004 the disease affected 80 per cent of Brazil's soybean area, with an estimated loss in value of yield of US $1 billion. The disease appeared to spread rapidly to eight US states, possibly exacerbated by the close genetic relatedness of the USA's soybean varieties, particularly in the south. The cost of conserving biodiversity is far outweighed by the huge cost of losses and chemical controls necessary to control major outbreaks of plant diseases. Increased diversity would offer some protection against soybean rust – of particular value to farmers who can't afford sprays. Although we can't predict the next disease, the solution lies in biodiversity conserved in gene banks or farmers' fields.

Mixed cropping systems still survive in many parts of the world, such as Mexico, where maize, beans, squash and peppers are grown together in the same plots. Many believe that the wider biodiversity of these mixed cropping systems offers increased protection from disease. A mixed cropping system can be seen in the West Africa section in the Humid Tropics Biome.

Some examples of mixed cropping systems have been established in the UK. In one system alley cropping strips, wide enough for machine cultivation, are surrounded by hedges of different species for fuel, food and materials.

The hedges form a barrier that protects the crops against pests, diseases and wind and traps extra heat which benefits early crops. Biodiversity helps to reduce pests. The hedges, for example, are a haven for beneficial animals that eat pests. Clover mixtures and other legumes are also used in the crop rotation to build up soil fertility and mixed varieties of crops such as wheat and potatoes are grown to reduce pests and diseases.

Challenges – war and natural disasters

Political instability and war can also lead to loss of crop biodiversity. Russian scientists starved to death rather than eat their genetic resources in the siege of Stalingrad during the Second World War.

Recent conflicts and civil strife resulted in the loss of seed collections in Liberia, Congo, Rwanda and Afghanistan.

In 1994 in Rwanda a million people were killed and two million people were displaced. The war had a serious effect on agriculture, in which 90 per cent of Rwanda's population are involved. A coalition of international help formed the 'Seeds of Hope' campaign to source and multiply traditional crop varieties lost in the fighting, introduce improved varieties and train agricultural extension workers. Since Rwanda has one of the richest diversities of common beans in the world, the loss of varieties during the war highlights the importance of duplicating collections held in other genetic resource centres.

Natural disasters such as the tsunami that hit South-east Asia in 2004 and Hurricane Mitch which battered Honduras and Guatemala in 1998 also affect plant communities and crops. In the case of Hurricane Mitch a 'Seeds of Hope' consortium formed of CGIAR Genetic Resource Centres and their partners sourced, multiplied and reintroduced lost crops and provided advice on reducing future risks. At the time of writing it is too soon to say for certain, but it can be assumed that similar initiatives will be brought to bear on devastated areas of South-east Asia.

A GM challenge

Mexico is part of the North American Free Trade Association (NAFTA), a regional trade association of Mexico, the USA and Canada. Mexico is also the centre of diversity for maize. In 2001 the Mexican government announced that traditional varieties of maize grown by farmers in the state of Oaxaca had become contaminated by transgenic sequences from imported North American maize. There was also concern about the possible contamination of teosinte (*Zea mays* subsp. *mexicana*), the wild ancestor of maize. There was a divergence of views subsequent to this between the government, who wanted to lift the ban on GM trials, and opponents who wanted a continuous ban. But this hasn't helped a poor, ageing farming population worried about simply surviving, and now negative publicity around GM maize means that they aren't sure if their maize is safe. This concern may speed up the abandonment of their land. There are concerns about biosafety if a range of GM varieties are grown; rules drawn up for developed countries will not necessarily work in the developing world where a culture of seed exchange exists. Studies by the International Maize and Wheat Improvement Center (CIMMYT) concluded that farmers' practices and incentives for growing traditional varieties affect maize genetic diversity far more significantly than the introduction of scientifically improved varieties of any type. GM crops could benefit a lot of people, but the effects of GM in centres of diversity need to be carefully considered.

International agreements

The original concept established by the United Nations Food and Agriculture Organization (FAO) was for free global exchange of genetic resource material around the world – as the common heritage for humanity. In the 1960s plant breeders' rights, providing for royalties to be paid on clearly identified new varieties to breeders only, led to concerns about ownership and benefit sharing. More than 174 countries

have now signed up to the Convention on Biology Diversity (CBD), originally ratified at the Earth Summit in Rio de Janeiro in 1992. CBD has three main goals: the conservation of biological diversity; its sustainable use; and fair and equitable sharing of benefits arising from the use of biological resources. The treaty also allows countries to consider genetic resources as national resources over which they have sovereignty.

The International Treaty on Plant Genetic Resources for Food and Agriculture, built on the CBD, came into force in 2004 when forty governments ratified it. It aims to develop an easy-to-use system, initially for access to thirty-five food crops and eighty fodder crops. The treaty is based on bilateral agreements between member countries. A benefit-sharing fund is being established for commercialized products resulting from the use of genetic resources. Payments are mandatory if the material is not available for further research, or voluntary if it is. In-trust agreements with the FAO were signed in 1994 by the CGIAR Centres, who placed their collections of genetic resources 'in trust' for the benefit of humanity. They waived any claim for ownership of intellectual property rights from all developments that use the genetic resources. Such claims have also to be waived by any recipients of the genetic resources, who receive a standard FAO-approved material transfer agreement. Unfortunately the treaty doesn't cover all crops; soybean is a case in point. Although countries are free to provide genetic resources of crops not listed, they are not legally obliged to do so. In the case of soybeans, this could slow down efforts to improve resistance to Asian soybean rust.

Who owns crop diversity?

In recent years there has been growing concern about ownership of crop biodiversity developed over millennia by local farmers – particularly when crops have been patented in the developed world. For example, a small yellow bean that appears to have originated in a bag of beans obtained from Mexico has been patented in Colorado. This has disrupted exports of yellow beans to the USA from Mexico, where they have been grown for millennia. Small-scale farmers in Colorado have been sued by the patent holder.

Greenpeace's International Genetic Engineering campaign highlighted a patent application by Monsanto covering a molecular marker in wild soya beans which can identify high-yielding varieties. The patent appears to apply to all plants wild and domesticated containing the marker, methods of screening for the markers and any breeding methods used with them. The opinion in southern China is that the plant material at the centre of the controversy is a result of generations of selection by local farmers. Monsanto say the patent only covers the technology in the USA, which has so far not ratified the Convention on Biological Diversity.

Top of the tree?

'Yes, we understand that we evolved over billions of years along with other species. We understand that most of the species that ever lived have become extinct. But do we understand that species continue to evolve? That evolution does not just apply to the past, but must also apply to the future? That Homo sapiens is not necessarily the highest and best evolution can do?'

Alanna Mitchell, *Dancing at the Dead Sea*

Biodiversity – food for thought

The plant kingdom is always in a slow but steady state of change, natural forces pushing and pulling the factors that influence adaptation, evolution and extinction.

The rate of change is accelerating, possibly because of our actions. In 1992 1,500 of the world's most prominent scientists, under the name of the Union of Concerned Scientists, issued a statement: 'Our massive tampering with the world's interdependent web of life – coupled with the environmental damage inflicted by deforestation, species loss and climate change – could trigger widespread adverse effects, including unpredictable collapses of critical biological systems whose interactions and dynamics we only imperfectly understand … we must recognize the Earth's limited capacity to care for us.' In essence we are creating an environment that may not be able to support us. Our dependence on biodiversity is beyond question – it sustains us in an unimaginable number of ways.

Most of us know all this. We know species are becoming extinct, we know the climate is changing, so do we really believe that our environment will just put up with it and support more and more of us every year? Do we believe that someone else is going to sort it out? Or do we just feel powerless to do anything?

Some believe that conserving biodiversity is a case of looking at the way we live, our core beliefs, and finding a way of changing it. This has happened many times in our history: when people realized that the world was not flat and when they accepted Darwin's theory of evolution, to give a couple of examples. It can happen again.

One of the great challenges of nature conservation for the twenty-first century is to work out how we can afford to save that which we cannot afford to lose. Somehow we have to learn to develop an economic system that does not rely on cashing in on existing biodiversity and that preferably actively pays back to sustain the core resource.

We need to live within the capacity of the global environment that we are part of, and realize that we can and do make a difference by the way we live, the way we consume, the way we communicate and by the way we look to nature for assistance. It's not just the way we treat our environment, either. The planet and the life on it will continue to evolve, with or without us. The way we behave towards each other is a key component for our future success.

At Eden we have shown, albeit on a small scale, that things can change. The transformation of the pit shows, for example, that degraded landscapes can be regenerated. The biodiversity conservation projects we have shown here and on our site are just the tip of the iceberg; there are thousands, possibly millions, across the world.

Biodiversity is important to us because of the products it supplies now, and will supply in the future. Protecting plants and animals in nature reserves, especially in hotspots, protects the potential, but it does nothing to protect the services (see page 159) and less tangible benefits (such as the joy of beauty) that most of us receive from nature even when we live far from the very special places. Another great challenge is therefore to find a system for biodiversity protection that is rather more sophisticated than creating reserves. Somehow we need to find room for people and nature to coexist, if only out of self-interest.

The philosophical model of conservation that dominated in the twentieth century was a reaction to a world where the richness of nature was degraded, if not entirely undermined, by human presence and activity. Today we are increasingly aware that human activity can coexist with, and even foster, diversity. This is true of traditional farming systems that produced the prairies of North America and the grasslands and heathlands of Europe. It is probably true of much of the tropical rainforests, which were once believed to be pristine and undisturbed but in reality show a huge history of human impact. Paradoxically it is also becoming true of real undisturbed systems such as tropical islands, where the consequences of human arrival have been devastating for the endemic plants and animals, but where human support and restoration of those systems now presents the only hope of avoiding more extinctions. In many cases the most serious threat to the maintenance of biodiversity in a region is not the presence of human activity; but that it may disappear. One of the side-effects of an intensified and more competitive global food system is that many traditional farming techniques are disappearing.

Perhaps the greatest challenge of nature conservation is to develop systems, and, more fundamentally, philosophies and policies that cherish and sustain human inputs of the right sort.

Of course there are also some places we should just leave alone – free to become whatever they want to become. Once again these pose a philosophical and policy challenge. Biodiversity is not static – one of the defining qualities of a rich and vibrant natural world is that it has the potential to respond to, and sometimes to moderate, environmental fluctuations. Climate change will lead to changes in what species live where. The final great challenge, therefore, is to find more flexible systems of responding to shifts in species distribution and behaviour. In a changing world, natural systems will no longer be restricted to the species and patterns that we are accustomed to. Conservation cannot be about resisting all change or else it becomes a futile King Canute exercise. There are no magic answers to these questions. Nature conservation is not about scientific and technical 'truths', it is about what we value and why we value it. We can only find the answers to those questions through more debate and engagement with the issues.

Darwin had it right: it is not the strongest species that survive, nor the most intelligent, but the ones most responsive to change.

Food

A visit to any supermarket presents us with a diversity of riches gathered from the four corners of the world. In the developed world, at least, we are privileged as no previous generation on Earth has ever been. At the same time no generation has ever been as ignorant about where this food comes from, how it is produced or even what it is we are putting into our mouths.

The movement of food around the world has a fascinating history. At its best, trading enriches and builds bridges between cultures. At its worst, it causes envy and hostility and leads to violence. Sometimes trade has sown the seed of traditions that have lasted for hundreds or thousands of years. To make buns Cornish bakers still use saffron, a Mediterranean spice that was originally traded for Cornish tin a thousand years ago. More recent change has transformed entire cuisines. Where would Italian food be without the tomato or 'traditional' British food without the potato? Yet both were unknown in Europe before the discovery of the Americas.

Some foods have had an even more profound impact because they have shaped entire economies and societies, and not always for the better. If you understand the history of trade in spices, sugar, coffee and tea, you understand half the political map of the world.

Issues concerning food trade are just as potent today. The energy used to transport fresh produce across the globe (food miles) is thought to be a major contributor to climate change. Many farmers in developing countries grow food for export rather than growing food for themselves, which makes economic sense in the short term … but not necessarily in the long term. The ease with which food can be moved around the world also throws into stark relief the problems of food shortages and malnutrition in developing countries. Flying in food aid patches the wound but does nothing to solve the underlying problems.

Scientists and agronomists are investigating ways to improve food security. For example, tissue culture techniques to produce new types of high-yielding rice, genetic fingerprinting to identify desirable traits in plants for the future and genetic modification to produce higher yields and disease resistant crops. Some applaud these technological advances while, paradoxically, others accuse them of undermining food supply and security.

GM has been one of the most rapidly adopted agricultural technologies and one of the most publicly debated. For example, people question whether GM:

- improves food supply for poor people or pushes them onto marginal land
- favours agribusiness and monoculture or the small farmers
- benefits or harms the health of the consumer
- has the potential to be clouded by vested interest
- is cost effective when compared to other technologies
- improves or is detrimental to biodiversity and the environment.

GM is only the latest manifestation of a move to more industrialized farming that is responsible for many undesirable trends. Even if it went away tomorrow, we would still be faced with concerns about chemicals and safety, the degradation of soil, the loss of wildlife habitats, excessive energy use in farming systems and the stories that we hear in the media about issues such as bird flu and CJD. Most of these issues are arguably connected to the way we farm.

In the West a root cause of many of these problems is the drive for ever-cheaper food, and an obsession with having every type of food available at every time of year. Thought needs to be given to whether we are really saving money by buying cheaply, or whether there are hidden costs that will adversely affect us in other ways. We also need to think about why we want to remove all seasonality from food supply.

Globally, however, there is a much more fundamental challenge – that of producing enough food to support the growing population, and the growing standard of living of much of that population. The need to feed additional billions in the coming decades could push food production systems to their limit, and we may be grateful for every technological advance we can muster. Sustainable husbandry techniques are also high on the agenda and include social as well as scientific propositions such as involving farmers in developing countries in the decision-making processes.

Among the food exhibits at Eden the key displays are of what we call 'the big six'. These are some of the most important staple foods that sustain the majority of the world's population today: wheat, potatoes, maize, pulses, bananas and rice. Feeding the developing and developed world alike, they are of immense importance, economically, socially, politically and environmentally. The section then goes on to explore other crops, vegetables, fruits, oils, drinks and flavourings. Food and health go hand in hand and their relationship is touched on here before being more fully explored in the health chapter.

Food is not just about sustenance and health. Running through most societies is an almost sacred belief that 'breaking bread' together as a family or 'feasting' as a community or intertribal gathering is a symbol of peace or fellowship. This is borne out by the hospitality that is expressed in all the great religions and cultures, but which is decreasing in our society. Here we want to remind ourselves of the role food plays in our lives, celebrate food and look to the future.

'Food is our common ground, a universal experience.'   James A. Beard

Bananas can be harvested to provide income all year round

Wheat

Wheat is the most commonly cultivated plant on the planet, occupying the largest area of the 'big six' globally, and has been adapted to grow in a wide range of conditions and climates. Around 95 per cent of it is *Triticum aestivum*, known as bread wheat. Almost a third of the world's people depend on bread. There are now over twenty thousand cultivars of bread wheat, including modern improved varieties and landraces (see page 15). As well as bread, cake and biscuits, wheat is used to make noodles (in China) and wheat tortillas (in Mexico). Just under 5 per cent of the world's wheat is *Triticum turgidum* subsp. *durum,* used for pasta. Other minor wheat species, such as spelt, can be found in cereals and health food shops.

The Green Revolution

This term describes a period of rapid technological advance in the production of staple foods which started in the 1960s, an advance that resulted in, for example, a sixfold increase in wheat production and a threefold increase in rice production in India alone in the following forty years. This prevented famine and disaster in much of the world at a time of rapid population increase. The achievement is not without its critics, who argue that it also laid the foundation of an approach to agriculture that has hidden social and environmental costs.

The revolution began in 1944, when Norman Borlaug, known as the father of the Green

A challenge for Europe

Over the past thirty years food has been getting cheaper and farmers have been getting a lower farm-gate price for their grain. To alleviate this they have grown higher-yielding varieties. European Union subsidies fixed to the production of commodities such as wheat are also coming to an end, so some farmers are considering changing their crops. Finding alternative uses for a crop, for instance as a source of a biofuel (see page 219), could also provide an alternative market in the future. If processing plants for biofuels gets the green light, it could help to reduce our use of petrol.

Once the price of wheat and bread depended on the success of the harvest. Today it is more complex with demand for exports being affected by global exchange rates and cheap imports competing with home-grown grains.

Revolution, was appointed as wheat breeder at the institute in Mexico, which later became the International Maize and Wheat Improvement Centre (CIMMYT). After the Second World War a dwarf wheat line brought over from Japan, 'Norin 10', was crossed with tall high-yielding wheat from the USA to develop a range of high-yielding, semi-dwarf wheat varieties, the first of which was released in 1961. Less energy went into growing stalks, so more went into producing grains. Short stems also helped to stop the plants from falling over. On the other hand the semi-dwarf wheat didn't suppress weeds as well as the tall types, so herbicides were needed. Borlaug was awarded the 1970 Nobel Peace Prize for developing these wheat strains and introducing those plants, along with improved farming practices, to hunger-plagued Third World countries, saving millions worldwide from starvation in the 1960s.

As the Green Revolution continued, the production of wheat and other staple crops soared. In India alone wheat production went from 10 million tonnes in 1964 to 70 million tonnes in 1999, simultaneously saving the country from mass famine and allowing the population to expand. Since the mid-1960s, even though the human population has increased to six billion, the majority are better fed, even though the area farmed has barely increased. The development of Green Revolution crops coincided with increased availability of fertilizers, herbicides and pesticides and irrigation, all of which contributed to increasing yields. The cost of these inputs, economically and environmentally, was considerable. Also far fewer people were working on the land to produce the same amount of food, which had huge social consequences.

Why does wheat rise?

Bread wheat contains proteins called gluten which give flour dough its unique viscous elasticity. Introducing gas bubbles and baking results in a highly desirable product: leavened bread. The gas can be introduced by using bicarbonate of soda or yeast. Yeast breaks down the starch in the bread, releasing carbon dioxide. The action of yeast on wheat was probably discovered by accident, and thereafter a bit of the old dough was added to each new batch to keep it going. It was not until the seventeenth century that yeast itself was identified and not until the nineteenth that Louis Pasteur discovered that it caused fermentation.

After the revolution

One of the concerns of the Green Revolution was to improve disease resistance. With wheat this has now been achieved by, for example, breeding for rust resistance using wheat varieties from around the world. Each year drought strikes more than half the area sown to wheat in the developing world, and work is being done to produce wheat varieties with high-yielding potential that use resources, such as water, more efficiently and produce good yields under low-input cultivation.

Improving varieties alone is unlikely to increase production much more, across the board, so scientists are working with farmers on crop-management techniques to increase production and save labour, resources and money. Low-tillage farming, for example, and using crop residues as a mulch, leaves the soil undisturbed during planting and saves up to half the crop's water use. Less digging also means fewer weeds, saving fuel and herbicide costs.

Demand for wheat is still increasing. In the developing world consumption is increasing by 5 per cent per annum and it is predicted that by 2020 the developing world will be consuming over 60 per cent of the world's wheat. Wheat is increasingly being favoured in China and the Indian subcontinent.

Wheat is one of the most commonly cultivated plants on Earth – Slovakia (above) and Peru (below)

Once again, one of the greatest challenges facing humanity is to ensure that we can sustain larger harvests fast enough to keep pace with our expanding, ever more urbanized numbers – and to make sure that the hungry benefit.

Potatoes

The potato (*Solanum tuberosum*), a member of the *Solanaceae* family, has some very poisonous relatives such as henbane, thorn apple and deadly nightshade, and is also related to tomatoes and petunias. Three to five thousand landraces of potato with a wide range of flavours, textures and maturing times exist in its centre of origin and diversity, the Andes. Many commercial varieties have been developed using modern breeding worldwide, about one hundred and fifty of which are grown in Britain.

Potatoes are extremely nutritious, containing 2 per cent protein, sugar and vitamins B and C. They produce a higher yield of food more rapidly than cereals and require less labour. In terms of global tonnage, potatoes are the fourth most important food crop in the world after maize, wheat and rice. They were first cultivated

Potato flower – potatoes are related to deadly nightshade

A Colombian farm growing rare types of potatoes

83

in the highlands of the southern Andes of South America, their original home, about eight thousand years ago, and brought to Spain in 1570. It took 200 years of selection, however, to produce varieties that cope with the longer European day. In Europe the potato was at first eaten only by the nobility and was claimed to be an aphrodisiac. The masses were suspicious of plants that came out of the ground, suspecting that potatoes were unholy and unhealthy. By the nineteenth century, however, the potato was the staple food of industrial workers across Europe. An acre (0.4 hectares) of potatoes could support a family and their pig (which was killed to pay the rent) year round. The population boomed, mostly because families were better fed.

A blight on the landscape

Late blight (*Phytophthera infestans*), the world's most costly and devastating crop disease, reached Belgium and France from Mexico by way of the United States in 1844. The blight spread, causing havoc, famine and death from Ireland and the Scottish Highlands to Russia. In the mid 1800s in Ireland a million people starved to death in the famine and a million and a half emigrated as a result of the blight. The late blight common in Europe today is probably not a direct descendant of that causing the Irish famine, but rather was introduced from Mexico in the late 1970s. These 'new' strains are difficult to control and are resistant to several fungicides that were previously effective in halting the disease. To control blight worldwide would cost several billion dollars a year.

Looking after our potatoes

The International Potato Centre (CIP) was set up in Lima, Peru, in 1971 to safeguard the gene bank of varieties developed over millennia in the Andes, and the thousands of wild potato relatives, for use worldwide. There potatoes can be used to breed new varieties and to try to combat diseases such as blight. Since then potato production has tripled and potatoes are being grown from the temperate regions to the tropics. Production and consumption is on the up in developing countries. As grain yields level off and the world population continues to expand by more than a hundred million a year, it is likely that the potato will become increasingly important as a world food. Potential yields may be double those of grains in terms of food value but realization of those gains means applying new techniques that include planting resistant crop varieties and improving cultivation.

Potatoes are still a valuable domestic food crop in their original home, the high Andes. There, some types are freeze-dried to make *chuño*, a dried potato that can be stored. Local products such as crisps are also being developed to bring income to rural communities.

Maize

Maize (*Zea* spp.) is a super-converter, changing the sun's energy into sugar faster, and potentially producing more grains, than any of the other major staples. It is the most important world crop in terms of tonnes harvested. Over 60 per cent of world production is used for animal feed, a figure likely to increase as meat consumption rises in step with affluence in some developing countries. Maize still plays a major role as a staple food for humans, for example in Africa as maize porridge and Latin American countries as tortillas. Besides being made into cornflakes and popcorn, maize starches sheets, sweetens toothpaste and helps make over five hundred products, including acetone, glue, cakes, crayons, cosmetics, ice cream, fireworks, ink, marshmallows, mats, mustard, paints, plastics, silage, soaps, shoe polish and whisky. Bread can't be made from maize, though, because it does not contain enough gluten to rise.

New varieties have led to the tripling of maize production in west and central Africa since the mid-1980s. The development of early and extra-early maturing varieties has enabled maize production to expand into the Sudan savannah zone. It has been estimated that gains in maize production in this region are sufficient to feed forty million people annually. Quality Protein Maize, which has been developed for farmers in the developing world, has higher levels of the essential amino acids lysine and tryptophan. (Traditionally, in the New World, beans, amaranth and other crops grown with maize supplied these amino acids.) New research is attempting to enhance the micronutrient content of maize and thereby combat widespread diseases caused by a lack of vitamin A, which causes corneal blindness, and a lack of iron, which causes anaemia.

Nearly all modern hybrid seed comes from the industrialized world and is generally associated with commercial maize farming and a high input of fertilizers and irrigation rather than the subsistence farming of the developing world. Hybrids do not come true from seed, so farmers have to buy fresh seed every year. Scientists are trying to produce maize that reproduces asexually through seed to produce exact clones of the mother (which some wild grasses do). This would mean that poor farmers would be able to save their own seed and grow high-yielding, pest-resistant varieties.

Maize and the GM debate

In the 1980s agrichemical companies realized that genetic engineering (GM) could reduce the need for a range of herbicides and pesticides associated with industrial farming. A major development has been the insertion of genes from a common soil bacteria, *Bacillus thuringiensis*, into maize to make the plants resistant to the European corn caterpillar and to the herbicide glyphosate so that fields can be cleared of weeds by an overall spray. Genetically modified maize first went on sale in the USA in 1995 and by 2003 around 40 per cent of maize production in the USA was genetically modified. Genetically modified maize is the world's second most important GM crop after soybean.

Serious concerns about GM crops from some European Union member countries in 1999 led to a block on the authorization of all new GM products until a legal framework for their production could be established. This was contested by the USA, Canada and Argentina. At the time of writing GM is still a hot topic in Europe. Proponents suggest that in the case of maize economic advantages of GM maize are proportionate to the losses in non-GM varieties caused by the European corn borer caterpillar, arguing also that removing the need to monitor pests and spray insecticide decreases production

Attention to detail

Of all the discoveries Christopher Columbus and his crew brought back to Europe from Central America, maize may have been the most valuable food crop. However, if they had paid as much attention to the people and their culture as to the plant they could have learnt a great deal more.

- In Meso America maize was grown with beans and squashes in mixed cropping systems. Maize needs nitrogen, and beans fix nitrogen from the atmosphere (see page 88). The beans climb up the stems of maize. Squash grow on vines on the ground, their spreading leaves keeping down weeds and helping to retain soil moisture. It is an excellent partnership all round, saving on fertilizers and weeding.

- Aztec women used to cook maize in lime or wood ash to loosen the outer covering before grinding the kernels to make tortillas. Unfortunately this technique was not adopted in Europe and Africa, where some of the poor, who lived predominantly off this maize, developed pellagra, a deficiency disease linked to lack of niacin (vitamin B4). It has recently been discovered that lime and wood ash can help to release niacin from maize seeds.

risks for farmers. Some field trials in the UK of GM oilseed rape, sugar beet and maize showed that production of the first two adversely affected biodiversity whereas the GM maize seemed to be better for wildlife. However, other studies found that GM maize could cross-pollinate with non-GM maize, a serious risk for organic maize production. At the beginning of 2005 Britain remained GM crop-free.

The GM issue is also creating moral and ideological debate in the developing world. When Zambia was faced with famine caused by a drought in 2002, threatening a quarter of its twelve million population, it was offered GM maize from the USA as relief, but farmers were wary, feeling that accepting GM maize would affect their non-GM status when exporting to Europe.

Kenya, together with South Africa, has been in the vanguard of GM technology. Having developed a GM infrastructure and field trialling skills through work on sweet potatoes, it is now turning its attention to maize in order to combat losses caused by stem borers.

Witch weed

Maize in Africa is attacked by the parasitic plant purple witch weed (Striga hermonthica), which literally sucks the life out of the plants, costing $7 billion a year in lost crops.

Scientists have now bred high-yielding maize varieties that incorporate resistance to the pest, and other control measures include a herbicide seed treatment and the introduction of a fungus, harmless to humans but lethal to Striga.

Maize harvested by hand in Tanzania

Making food out of fresh air

We need nitrogen to make protein. The air is 78 per cent nitrogen, but we can't absorb it like this and neither can most plants. Peas and beans, however, can make protein from the air, or rather a type of bacteria called rhizobium that lives in their roots can. Each legume plant species has its own type of rhizobium. Legume plants allow the rhizobium to invade the plant roots, which develop lumps called nodules. The plant gives the rhizobium a home and sugar, and in return the rhizobium turns nitrogen from the air into plant food, given the right soil nutrition conditions. If you cut a root nodule in half you may notice that it is pink. That's because it contains leghaemoglobin, a plant equivalent of blood, essential for the efficient function of the 'root fertilizer factory'.

Edible legumes

We may regard peas as mushy and tinned beans as a fast food but these pulses and their close relations contain the building blocks of life. Pulses are the edible protein-rich members of the legume family (*Leguminosae*), which are easy to spot because they have pods and often have pea-like flowers and divided leaves. Seeds of legumes can be dried, stored and easily transported – and can increase soil fertility thanks to *Rhizobium* bacteria which can colonize their root systems and make nitrogen fertilizer out of nitrogen in the air, which is then converted into protein. Soybeans contain up to 38 per cent protein. Wheat, maize, rice and potato, though high in carbohydrates, contain less protein than pulses.

For some, pulses or grain legumes represent a choice of protein-rich food, from veggie burgers to soya milk and soya sauce. For some, they are a source of animal fodder. Some pulses or grain legumes represent a means of survival and potential escape route from poverty for farmers in the developing world, a means of survival particularly for farmers outside the cash economy, where the complementation of pulse crops and cereals provides much of the essential nutrition for life.

Know your beans

Soya (*Glycine max*) produces 60 per cent of the world's animal feed and a fifth of the world's vegetable oil, and is found in about 70 per cent of our supermarket products.

The circular irrigation pattern of a Brazilian soya field

The USA grows half the world's soybeans and about forty million Chinese farmers rely on soya for their livelihoods. The low incidence of breast and colon cancer in China and Japan and the lack of menopausal symptoms in women has been partly attributed to the high consumption of soya. However, in 2004 reports showed that the high levels of oestrogens found in soya may have a detrimental effect on health for some.

Soybeans, bred to grow in cooler northern climates, were the result of a school genetics class held in a public park in Minsk. The idea was to find an alternative to expensive imports for landlocked Belarus. A UK seed company agreed to commercialize one or more of the varieties produced and to pay royalties to the breeder. One variety, 'Northern Conquest', now grows on farms in southern England, and at Eden.

Lentil (*Lens culinaris*), among the earliest plants to be domesticated by humans, has recently been developed for the dry areas of western Asia. Scientists in the seventeenth century named the convex glass they had invented a lens because it resembled the shape of a lentil.

Chickpea (*Cicer arietinum*) got its name, which means 'ram-like', from the Romans. Some think the seeds also resemble chicks' heads. An important crop in North Africa, Asia and Mexico, chickpeas make up the largest share of the Middle East's legume production. Chickpeas need little input in terms of labour and fertilizers, are drought-resistant, and can produce two crops a year.

Baked bean or navy bean (*Phaseolus vulgaris*) is an example of the common bean,

A variety of pulses on display in a Sicilian market

which originally came to Europe from Mexico. European settlers took them back to New England in the eighteenth century, and they were carried as rations by early travellers and prospectors in the USA. Sacks of navy beans were ideal nautical food when stored dry, as their hard seed coat didn't sprout in the damp. These beans were later canned as cheap nutritious food for the armed forces, and their appearance in US military rations during the Second World War helped to establish the baked bean as an important part of the UK diet.

Cowpea (*Vigna unguiculata*), from Africa, is now consumed by 200 million people across the tropics and subtropics. Often known as the crop of the poor, it is drought tolerant, adapted to grow on poor soils, and shade tolerant, which means it can be grown between other crops, saving space and resources.

Pigeon pea (*Cajanus cajan*), from India, is grown as a smallholder's crop in semi-arid and tropical regions of the world. It is often used to make dhal.

Toxic food!

Beans do have an Achilles heel. A few are toxic, containing 'anti-nutritional compounds', which prevent them from being eaten in the wild. Some of these compounds cause indigestion and wind, others can kill. Toxin levels can be reduced by breeding and, in some cases, by preparation techniques such as soaking and correct cooking.

Grass peas (*Lathyrus sativus*) are a staple crop in Ethiopia, India and Pakistan and can survive times of drought when many other crops fail. These peas are harmless if they form less than a third of the diet and are eaten for only three to four months of the year. Beyond this level they can cause a permanent paralysis called lathyrism. This is particularly a problem for young working men and for bonded labourers in India and Pakistan, who were sometimes paid in grass peas. The International Centre for Agricultural Research in Dry Areas has now bred grass peas with low toxin levels that can be eaten without fear of paralysis.

Since the 1960s scientists and nutritionists, ranging from those working to feed astronauts to those developing food for babies in Uganda, have been on the lookout for a non-flatulent bean. Meanwhile in Chile, Mexico and Peru people chose to eat more digestible traditional yellow bean varieties. In the 1980s, thinking that colour might provide a clue to the problem, Colin Leakey, Friend of Eden, bred a new yellow cultivar from northern temperate parents called 'Prim'. He also developed and tested a portable flatometer to carry out controlled measurements of windiness, which showed that his new beans were better than his control varieties, and no more wind-inducing than muesli!

Bananas

The banana (*Musa* spp.) is not a tree; its stem is made of leaves, not wood. The largest species can grow 30 metres tall – not bad for a herb! Most edible bananas are seedless and sterile, and the stem dies after harvesting. New shoots grow from the base of the old one; they can yield fruit within a year and be used to propagate new plants. There are about a thousand types of banana: sweet, savoury, round, bent, straight, green, yellow, pink, silvery and even spotted and striped. Bananas can be harvested all year round, thus providing a steady stream of income. They also take only nine months to recover after a hurricane, unlike tree crops, which take years.

This high-energy food feeds some four hundred million people in the developing world. Uganda, Burundi and Rwanda consume around 250 kilograms per person per year, the highest consumption in the world. Bananas are rich in carbohydrates, potassium, phosphorus, calcium, iron and vitamins A, B and C.

Originally from South-east Asia and the western Pacific, bananas still grow wild in the Philippines, Papua New Guinea and Indonesia. Popolou, a type spread by Polynesian people five thousand years ago, has been grown at Eden. Scientists have recently become interested in one variety, 'Karat', which has orange-fleshed fruit rich in beta carotene, often in short supply in diets in the developing world.

In the UK we eat around 130 bananas each a year. Europe has always supported the traditional small farms in the African, Caribbean and Pacific (ACP) countries relying heavily on banana exports to survive. This led to the 'banana wars', a dispute which brought a ruling from the World Trade Organization that Europe should reduce its economic support for the ACP. The upshot tended to favour larger farms that can produce cheaper fruit, though often at the expense of incomes and working conditions. Up to the early 1990s 60 per cent of the UK banana requirement came from the Windward Islands, but this has since fallen to less than 20 per cent.

Many Caribbean bananas are produced on small family-owned farms on steep volcanic hillsides with low inputs of fertilizers and chemicals and low investment all round. The bananas are often the only source of income and need constant attention. Small packing stations have been established to ensure that bananas are transported via refrigerated ships and ripening stores to arrive on shop shelves without bruises. Fortunately the islands' bananas do not suffer from black sikatoka disease, which leads to a yield reduction of up to 70 per cent. In Latin America bananas have to be sprayed up to forty times a year to ward off this disease. The Windward Islands Banana Development & Exporting Company (WIBDECO) is a not-for-profit organization, owned by the farmers, and all the profits associated with transport distribution and marketing of bananas under WIBDECO's control flow back to the farmers. Caribbean banana farmers cannot compete with their Latin American counterparts on price but they can attract a premium by trading under the Fairtrade logo (see opposite), for example.

Commercial bananas in Central America are usually produced on cleared rainforest plantations or flat land owned by corporates or governments. Generally production is large-scale, fertilizer and chemical inputs are high and there is money to reinvest. Workers can be poorly paid and their health put at risk from the use of chemicals. Production is sometimes shifted from one country to another to reduce costs. There are examples of good practice in Latin America, however. The Earth University in Costa Rica has been developing more sustainable systems of producing bananas.

Fairtrade bananas

Fairtrade bananas, first sold in Britain in 2000, have rapidly grown in popularity and by 2004 represented 4 per cent of sales. When we buy a Fairtrade banana, more of the purchase price goes to the grower. The Fairtrade deal includes:

- direct trade with growers, cutting out local middlemen
- guaranteed prices to cover production costs
- payment of a premium for social and environmental improvement
- credit
- long-term agreements to allow farmers to plan ahead.

Fairtrade bananas and other Fairtrade products are available in most supermarkets.

The organic banana market is tiny and demand from the developed world is currently outstripping supply. The organic market is beneficial to small-scale farmers who have not been able to afford to use chemical inputs but many farmers need help through the initial steps of entering it. Development projects can help with organic conversion and market development, while agreements with large multinational banana firms have allowed farmers to sell their bananas at a fixed price, so providing some security. There are longer-term concerns, however, about profitability when supplies of organic bananas match market demand.

There is currently international controversy over impending changes to the EU banana import regime. Until 1 January 2006, bananas can continue to be imported into the EU from Latin America at a reduced tariff of 75 euros up to a quota limit of about 3 million tonnes, while imports from certain African and Caribbean (ACP) countries enter duty-free under a quota of 750,000 tonnes. But under agreements between the EU and the USA and Ecuador that settled a long-running dispute in the WTO, those quotas are to end. There will be a higher tariff on Latin American bananas, designed to provide an equivalent degree of protection to ACP producers, but with no limits on the volumes imported. This is proving highly controversial. The Caribbeans fear that with the removal of quotas, their small family industry will rapidly be forced out of the market by the large-scale Latin American plantations. The Latin Americans fear that any increase in the tariff will give an unfair advantage at their expense to African producers, whose bananas will continue to enter duty-free. Some believe that the fairest solution for all would be to leave things exactly as they are. As a consumer you play a role in the future of this industry.

Mouldy bananas

In the early twenty-first century a new problem has hit the banana industry: a strain of a fungal disease called Panama disease that attacks root systems. This has already cut banana production in Uganda by 40 per cent and could have the same devastating impact on subsistence farmers as the Irish potato famine. Cuban farmers have also suffered serious losses because they are unable to afford fungicides. They are now planting modern varieties that are resistant to fungal disease but taste different from their traditional banana varieties.

Before the Second World War the main export banana from the tropics was 'Gros Michel'. When this variety succumbed to Panama disease, different forms of the 'Cavendish' took its place. Now 'Cavendish' is beginning to suffer from a new strain of Panama disease. The search to find or breed a disease-free replacement is complicated by the need to find one that also appeals to consumer tastes and fits into 'established' production systems.

The Future Harvest Centre, International Network for the Improvement of Banana and Plantain, has a collection of over a thousand different banana types held 'in trust' for the public good which may be used in breeding programmes. It deep freezes (cryopreserves) this precious plant material for future use. Now the banana is to become the first fruit to have its genome (genetic blueprint) sequenced, by a public consortium of scientists from eleven countries, offering the opportunity to develop bananas not only with resistance to disease but of varying taste. As bananas are difficult to breed conventionally, GM technology could be an option for incorporating specific useful characteristics. Provided these fruits remain sterile, there is no chance of the newly integrated genes getting into wild relatives or weeds.

Rice

Rice (*Oryza* spp.) is fundamental to many cultures. It has fed more people over a longer time than any other crop. Today it is the number-one food crop, feeding around half the people in the world.

Rice is grown as far north as Manchuria and as far south as Uruguay, but has a special significance in South and South-east Asia, where the words 'rice' and 'food' are synonymous. Recent archaeological finds in South Korea and China suggest that rice may have been cultivated there over eleven thousand years ago.

The Green Revolution (see page 80) boosted rice yields considerably. The first semi-dwarf, high-yielding rice, 'IR8', was launched by the International Rice Research Institute in 1966. Since then many rice varieties have been bred. There is still a need to increase rice production in Asia to provide rice for its population, which is expected to reach approximately 5.5 billion (around 60 per cent of the world's total) by 2050. The main problems now are uneven distribution and inadequate resources.

As well as yield increases there is now more emphasis on improving human nutrition through dietary diversification and enhancing micronutrients in existing crops. Current research activities are looking to improve the content of zinc, iron, vitamin A (beta carotene in its plant form) and essential elements in the rice grain. Increasing levels of beta catotene in rice grain – producing golden rice – requires genetic engineering as this micronutrient is not naturally found in rice grains. Suitable lines (cultivars of the future) that have passed all biosafety checks will not be available for some years yet.

Until recently rice prices have shown greater stability than those of wheat and maize, which has helped poor communities, such as landless workers and the growing urban populations who spend a high proportion of their income on food. In recent years, many governments in rice-producing countries have intervened to keep food rice prices high to benefit farmers. Only

The rice harvest in Madagascar

The world of rice

Asia: *nearly 90 per cent of the world's rice is produced in the Far East. In industrial countries such as Japan and South Korea consumption is falling because of an increasing demand for wheat and Western fast foods.*

Australia: *one of the most hi-tech rice producers.*

Africa: *rice consumption is increasing. New higher-yielding rice varieties have been developed, enabling farmers to produce a surplus that they can sell.*

South America: *rice is an important staple in this area, especially in Brazil, Colombia and Peru.*

Near East: *Egypt is the largest producer in the Near East. Iran has a long history of rice consumption.*

Europe: *Italy is the largest rice producer and Portugal the greatest consumer.*

USA: *The USA is one of the world's top four rice exporters. Production is highly mechanized; satellite tracking sets up the rice fields and aeroplanes sow the seed.*

about 6 per cent of the world's production of rice is traded globally, the main exporters being Thailand, Vietnam, India and the USA. In 2004, after five years of declining production, China started to import rice to meet the shortfall caused by increased industrialization, water shortages and farmers opting to grow higher-value crops. The effect has been an increase in the world price for rice, benefiting exporters but not importers.

Asian rice farmers have, on average, half an acre of land each. Since this is more than is needed to feed a family, substantial quantities of rice enter commercial marketing channels inside each country. However, income often has to be supplemented by non-agricultural jobs. In Bangladesh a UK initiative (a Department for International Development project) has encour-aged small-scale farmers to produce fast-growing young tilapia, a type of fish, in their rice paddies. The fish aerate and enrich the soil, and eat pests and rice residues after harvest. The farmers benefit from the extra income and the diversity of food and are less likely to use harmful pesticides on their rice in case it harms their fish. Eden have been working with Stirling University and people in Bangladesh who are involved in this initiative to tell their story to the public.

The future

Rice is a thirsty crop: on average 3,000 litres of water are needed to produce 1 kilogram of rice. Friction already exists between the growing urban settlements, industry and agriculture over water usage. In China irrigated rice production is banned around Beijing because of water shortages and the Yellow River no longer reaches the sea because of over-extraction of water. Scientists are developing 'aerobic rice', which makes better use of water and does not require paddies. Climate change is also starting to affect the rice crop, with yields dropping as temperatures rise above a certain point.

The current challenge is to grow higher-yielding rice on a decreasing area of available farmland that uses resources more efficiently. To meet future needs scientists are also working to try to breed rice with desirable characteristics including:

- lower flower head height to reduce shading, allowing leaves to intercept more sunlight
- fewer stems supporting more productive flower heads
- stiff, short flower stems to reduce bending under the weight of seeds
- ability to use water and nutrients efficiently.

To do this they have to turn to the smallholders and subsistence farmers who have been developing their own rice landraces over the years, in the hope that one of them will hold the key (the genes) to future success.

One solution is hybrid rice, first developed in China, which can outyield conventional varieties by 20–30 per cent. Hybrid rice occupies 50 per cent of Chinese rice production area, which is responsible for 60 per cent of the total rice production. The technology is spreading to other countries such as India, the Philippines, Vietnam, the USA and Bangladesh where, in total, 1.5 million hectares of hybrid rice were planted in 2004. In China, thousands of farmers have been able to grow their traditional disease-susceptible rice varieties by interplanting them with hybrid rice without resorting to fungicides – a successful use of crop biodiversity.

Rice terraces near Sapa, close to the Chinese border in northern Vietnam

Minor grains

The so-called 'minor grains' feed millions. Many are grown by subsistence farmers who live 'on the edge'. All these minor grains have within them the potential to be developed to suit different climatic conditions. They have a great deal to offer in terms of food security in the face of the increasing threat of drought and climate change, as well as offering considerable health benefits in the developed world.

Millet Many different grain species are referred to as millet: pearl millet (*Pennisetum glaucum*) from West Africa, finger millet (*Eleusine coracana*) from East Africa, and common (*Panicum miliaceum*) and foxtail millets (*Setaria italica*) from eastern Asia. All are rich in B vitamins, calcium, iron and potassium. Unlike wheat, millets are gluten free, and therefore very useful for coeliacs. Today over five hundred million people depend on pearl millet as their primary food source.

Tef (*Eragrostis tef*) is only a major crop in Ethiopia, its centre of origin. It still fills the basic dietary requirements for millions of people across eastern Africa, where the grain is milled into flour and made into injera, a flat bread, high in amino acids and iron. It even contains a natural yeast that allows the injera mix to ferment and adds extra vitamins as well. The word 'tef' comes from the Amharic word meaning 'lost', reflecting the small size of the seeds. It tolerates a wide range of growing conditions, from lowland to high altitudes and from dry semi-arid farmland to heavily waterlogged soils. Some is grown in other countries, including limited commercial production in South Africa and the USA.

Sorghum (*Sorghum bicolor*), an ancient food crop, was domesticated in the north-east quadrant of Africa between the Nile Valley and Lake Chad, Ethiopia. Like tef, it moved along trading routes from the Middle East to India, then by the silk route to China, where it is now a major crop.

Sorghum is also the third largest cereal crop in the USA, used in the manufacture of syrups, sugar, fibre and fuel. In Africa there is a resurgence of interest in developing drought-resistant varieties of sorghum to replace maize, which is poorly suited to the increasingly dry climate.

Quinoa (*Chenopodium quinoa*) is the most recently commercialized non-grass grain, high in protein, B vitamins, potassium and carbohydrates as well as being gluten free. Closely related to a British weed species called Fat Hen, quinoa has been cultivated for at least five thousand years. The Incas called it the 'mother grain' and regarded it as a sacred plant that spiritually enhanced its consumer. In the sixteenth century its cultivation became restricted because of Spanish attempts to destroy the crop, banning all Inca customs involving its use. It is now eaten as a health food in the USA and Europe and is made into flour for people allergic to gluten.

Winnowing millet in Mali

99

The origins of agriculture

Agriculture probably started independently in separate continents. The most detailed work exploring its origins has been carried out in the Fertile Crescent (modern-day Turkey, Jordan, Syria, Israel, Iraq and Iran). It is likely that agriculture was triggered by a change from a nomadic to a settled way of life, possibly linked to climate change, population growth or the casual cultivation of special plants near settlements. In Syria 11,000 years ago, for instance, people were hunting animals and gathering plants across the grassy steppes. They would have set up camps in fertile river valleys with plenty of water and wild food. Soon these became settlements of small groups related by kinship, who lived on a varied diet of over a hundred wild plant species and seeds collected and stored for lean times. Over time the climate became colder and drier and many of the wild species started to disappear, so the settlers probably began to clear ground and sow, plant and tend the most useful plants.

Such early farmers would have selected plants for a variety of reasons: because their grains stayed on the plant rather than fell off, and were plumper and more nutritious than others; or because they grew faster and stored better, and were not liable to go dormant. With this process evolution was given a helping hand, and certain plants began to fare very well. Humans have come to rely on domesticated crops for survival – and equally, the domesticated crops need humans for their survival. Domesticated maize has been around for more than 5,000 years, but can no longer disperse its own seed.

> *'History celebrates the battlefields wherein we meet our death, but scorns to speak of the ploughed fields whereby we thrive. It knows the names of the King's bastards but cannot tell us the origin of wheat.'*
>
> Jean-Henri Fabré

It took around 2,500 years for mature farming communities to replace hunting and gathering communities and a further 4,000 years for larger hierarchical communities to evolve. This evolution included the development of 'states', central control of agricultural hinterlands, use of irrigation, hierarchical structures, a more specialized workforce including artisans and priests, and markets, writing and weapons.

Originally hunting was thought to be mainly carried out by men, gathering by women. Agriculture was an extension of gathering, so women were more involved in early farming than men. Men became more involved when marketing developed in agriculture and with the introduction of heavy tools such as the plough. The development of agriculture led to a collapse in dietary diversity – from over a hundred plant species picked by gatherers to a handful of agricultural crops supplemented by fewer and fewer wild harvested plants.

Today women are still the world's main farmers

Vegetables

The vitamins, proteins, fibre and minerals found in vegetables provide us with an invaluable range of nutrients and other dietary requirements. As modern life in the West becomes more stressful, and with conditions like strokes, high blood pressure and obesity on the increase, vegetables are a way of maintaining good health. Research going back to the 1950s indicates that a healthy diet is based on fresh vegetables, fruit and grains, with smaller quantities of meat and dairy products than found in current Western diets. Notably, people in the Mediterranean regions of Europe have a low level of chronic disease and a longer life expectancy than in other developed countries, reflecting the greater proportion of vegetables, fruit and olive oil consumed there. Sadly even in these regions young people are turning their back on the local diet.

The Warm Temperate Biome at Eden grows a range of vegetables from the Mediterranean, California and South Africa, showing the importance of these climatic regions as the kitchen gardens of the world. Some of these places now support major industries, such as vast areas of tomatoes in California, and peppers under plastic in Greece and Spain. These intensively grown crops all need food, water and protection against pests and diseases. Pressure is mounting to reduce subsidies on water and to change to energy-efficient, self-sustaining and diversified farming, producing the kind of crops grown by a Greek or Spanish gardener fifty years ago.

Initiatives using low-cost, innovative technology such as the 'sea-water greenhouse' may help. This sustainable solution to providing fresh water to arid coastal regions uses sea water to cool and ventilate a large polytunnel, and sun to distil fresh water from sea water.

The range of vegetables that grace our tables and gardens has increased so dramatically that we are in danger of forgetting where the vegetables come from and what cost that might entail. A South African-grown carrot that gives us one unit of energy when we eat it used sixty-eight units when it was flown to us.

What to do? Growing your own or buying local could provide a couple of options.

Many of the world's poorer countries increase their exports to increase their foreign earnings and pay off debts. In some cases this means that land once used to grow food for

Harvesting tomatoes in California

home consumption has been turned over to high-value cash crops. This can lead to a spiralling dependence on others, vulnerability to changes in the global markets as well as nutritional problems. Vegetable production in Kenya has increased sixfold in the last thirty years but as much of this is for export it has led to a decrease in vegetable consumption by the local population.

Growing your own

In the UK At Eden our Plants for Taste exhibit grows a range of attractive vegetables all year round, encouraging our visitors to take up the fork in more ways than one. A bit of outdoor activity helps to keep you fit, not to mention the fresh produce at the end of it.

In Malaysia In the tropics the heat and humidity mean that vegetables don't travel well. Sometimes the vegetables grown are specific to that area and have been selected and grown by the local people for thousands of years. In the Humid Tropics Biome is a garden based on five smallholdings in Sabah, Malaysia. This *kebun* is a backyard 'self-sufficient larder' where local people have selected, collected and bred the best from the surrounding rainforest. The plants are tropical but there are similarities with our own gardens – fruit trees, herbs, flowers and vegetable beds. In the tropics winged beans and yard-long beans grow where we might grow runner or broad beans, helping to fertilize the soil; pak choi replaces cabbage and taro replaces carrots. The wide range of plants provides food security all year round. In times of drought or hardship there is always something to eat – guavas, mangoes, sweet potatoes and even the horseradish tree (*Moringa oleifera*), a leguminous tree with edible leaves, beans, flowers and roots that smell of horseradish, often used in soups. The garden also provides building materials, medicines and fruit to barter or sell at the local market.

In the city Soon over half the world's population may live in cities, partly because of the flight from the land to find work. Many, especially in developing countries, arrive in cities to find poverty and hunger rather than employment. One response has been an increase in urban food production. In Dar es Salaam, Tanzania, where 20 per cent of the workers are involved in urban agriculture, 90 per cent of the leafy vegetables eaten in the city are grown there. In Indonesia, during the financial crisis of 1998, the government encouraged Jakarta to grow its own food. Worldwide some eight hundred million city-dwellers grow some of their own food; 30 per cent of Russia's food is produced on urban land and thirty thousand Londoners have allotments. Urban agriculture increases food security as well as having social and environmental benefits.

Local sourcing

Local sourcing helps to reduce food miles and supports local economies. Farmers' markets are on the increase, and some supermarkets are beginning to follow the trend by supplying specialist foods in different regions. Eden sources 90 per cent of its catering supplies locally, and has opened up opportunities for new markets as part of Cornwall's regeneration programme.

Cornwall's maritime climate, influenced by the Gulf Stream, brings mild winters and relatively cool summers. Historically the climate, which is unlike that of the rest of the country, has allowed Cornish farmers to produce high-value crops such as early potatoes, winter cauliflowers and cabbages at times of shortage elsewhere in the UK. Today things are changing. The trend is towards larger farms, with smaller farms becoming part-time enterprises or 'hobby farms'. Supermarkets rather than regional markets buy the bulk of produce from the farmers. Competition from foreign imports increases year by year. Increased demand for local and seasonal food and awareness of food miles could help to turn the tables.

The Plants for Taste exhibit at Eden

Gardens for Life

A recent survey reported that 60 per cent of children in Scotland do not know that crisps come from potatoes. Food education for children is vital. Eden's Gardens for Life project is an international initiative involving the children of three continents growing food crops in school gardens. Starting with Kenya, India and the UK, Gardens for Life is setting up a network of voices, of children and teachers talking to each other about growing food. This enriches teaching and learning, improves health through growing and eating the fresh local vegetables they produce, and might also lay the basis for global action on urgent issues. Modern electronic communication between schools can make classrooms truly international, and the experience of growing vegetables in school gardens can bring children together in a unique conversation about what is necessary for the survival of humanity everywhere.

Fruit

The campaign to get us all to eat five portions of fruit and vegetables a day is well known, but even before it began fruit consumption was on the up; a rise of 55 per cent between 1975 and 2003. The phrase 'An apple a day keeps the doctor away' was coined in 1904 by J. T. Stinson, Director of the Missouri State Fruit Experimental Station. He lived to be ninety-two. Fruits contain a range of vitamins, minerals and natural chemicals that have been claimed to reduce heart disease, help to prevent certain cancers and even clean your teeth. The vitamin C content of fruit varies enormously; blackcurrants, kiwi and guava all contain over 100 mg per 100 g (the recommended daily allowance is 75–90 mg). Coming in with well over 1,000 mg is the West Indian cherry.

Tropical fruits such as star fruit and passion fruit have developed a fashion value much like that enjoyed by the pineapple in the eighteenth century when it became a status symbol on the dining table and in the greenhouse. Demand for such exotica has burgeoned, fed by advances in harvesting techniques, packaging and the high-speed movement of freight around the globe.

But what are the implications? As with vegetables, so with fruit: on the one hand such demand could mean increased income for smallholders and maintenance of rural communities in developing countries; on the other, increased food miles, competition with home-grown fruits, an increase in monocultures, possible environmental implications, the inability of local smallholders to compete with the larger growers, not to mention depriving local people of traditional nutritious foods. In some cases, export associations have stepped in to ensure that smallholders can meet legislative criteria and compete with the big players. Some fruit exporters provide transport, logistics and training to smallholders as well as economies of scale that make their produce more competitive.

A fruit seller in Halong Bay, Vietnam

New techniques that aim to reduce environmental damage from pesticides (which tend to be used on more intensive, monoculture systems) include organic production, intercropping and adoption of integrated pest management techniques using fewer chemicals. There are also moves to ensure socially responsible importing, with the growers receiving a fair deal and money going back to the countries of origin (see page 93). Eden grows a wide range of fruits from the tropics, Mediterranean and temperate regions of the world. Each has its own story.

Pineapples

Pineapples (*Ananas comosus*) were cultivated by the Tupi-Guarani Indians in South America thousands of years before being brought to Europe by the Spanish conquistadors. This tropical fruit is a perennial, and can live up to thirty years, although commercial production today tends to replace the plants after one season.

The first commercial plantation, established in Hawaii in 1885, produced most of the world's pineapples until the 1960s. The largest exporters of fresh pineapples today are Costa Rica, Côte d'Ivoire and the Philippines, while Thailand and the Philippines lead the processed pineapple trade. The scale of production is enormous. Fruits are mass-produced on farms hundreds of hectares in size, chemical controls being employed to deal with the range of pests and diseases that affect this monocultural crop.

The pineapple yields more than fruit. Industrial alcohol, made from the fruit sugars, can be mixed with ether and used in car engines. Juicing residues are used as livestock feeds because of their high vitamin A content. Bromelain, a protein-digesting enzyme prepared from pineapple wastes, is used for tenderizing meat, chill-proofing beer and treating inflammation, and is being investigated for thrombosis treatment.

Pineapples are one of the most intensively researched tropical fruit crops in the world. The future may see an increase in super-sweet types to satisfy modern taste buds. There is intense pressure to reduce pesticide usage, though breeding for pest and disease resistance has proved largely unsuccessful. Other strategies tried include genetic modification to control nematodes and mealy bugs. The challenge is to overcome pests and diseases using environmentally sound techniques.

Mangoes

In producing countries, mangoes (*Mangifera* spp.) are eaten savoury, sweet, pickled, salted, fresh or dried. They are high in fibre, potassium, iron and vitamins A, C and E. Dried mango flowers, seed kernel decoctions, leaves, bark, resinous gum from the trunk and unripe fruit are all used for traditional medicinal applications.

Mangoes for sale near Nha Trang, Vietnam

106

Native to the Himalayan regions of India and Myanmar, the mango is now cultivated throughout the tropics and some areas of the subtropics. Over four thousand years of selection has produced hundreds of different varieties in a range of sizes, shapes and colours. Many of the major export varieties have been bred in Florida.

One problem with exporting mangoes is the weight of the seed, sometimes 30 per cent of the weight of the whole fruit. One solution is to process the fruit, which has the benefit of adding value in the country of origin. Recent developments have seen fruit producers in the northern and southern hemispheres, whose mango seasons complement each other, co-operating on marketing.

Citrus

Most citrus fruits came originally from Southeast Asia, and were first cultivated in China and India. In the seventeenth century an orange was a scarce luxury item. Today 7 million hectares of citrus fruits are grown globally, irrigated with over 60 trillion litres of water.

The valleys of central California are now some of the most intensively farmed areas in the world. They rely heavily on irrigation from the snowmelt of the Sierra Nevada, competing with other water users. More water is needed on plantations being developed on drier land than in the river valleys where citrus trees have traditionally been grown. If not carefully controlled, watering can cause a build-up of salts in the soil, which reduces yields. California's huge levels of resource consumption and wealth accumulation have social and environmental costs. However, the region is also the birthplace of innovative new sustainable technology and home to some of today's most environmentally conscious people, searching for solutions to inherited problems.

Apples

The ancestors of our English apples (*Malus domestica*) came from a small area of central Asia, the Tien Shan, that runs from the borders of China, through Kazakhstan, into Kyrgysztan and part of Tajikistan, and to the west into

Citrus groves dominate the modern landscape of California

107

Uzbekistan. Small, endangered areas of intact 'Fruit Forest' apple trees, along with pear, plum, apricot and cherry, still survive in their centre of origin.

Monasteries played a role in improving apples during the Middle Ages, but breeding and selection started in earnest in the eighteenth century. By 1900 some two thousand varieties – 'Ribston Pippin', 'Peasgood's Nonesuch', 'Bloody Turk', 'D'arcy Spice' and 'Pitmaston Pineapple' to name but a few – were being grown in the UK to provide an almost year-round supply. 'Cox's Orange Pippin' and 'Bramley', both English varieties dating from the nineteenth century, are still in our shops, but have been joined by 'Braeburn', originally from New Zealand, 'Granny Smith' from South Africa and 'Golden Delicious' from France.

The UK may produce some of the tastiest apples in the world but its cooler climate leads to lower yields and higher costs than many other producing countries, for example France, South Africa and Argentina. In the last ten years two-thirds of the UK's apple growers have thrown in the towel, 15 per cent in 2001–2 alone. In 2005 European Union production subsidies for specific crops have been withdrawn and replaced with Single Farm Payments of around £200 a hectare. Under this scheme commercial orchards are designated as 'perennial' and will not be eligible for the payments, which threatens to be the last nail in the coffin. We lament the loss of jobs, traditional landscapes, local cultural heritage and flavour. Some growers are taking their diverse varieties to increasingly popular farmers' markets; others are making specialist juices and of course cider. The consumer does have a voice. Supermarkets may control the market, but they respond to our needs. We can ensure that that need is felt.

Cornish apple grower Mary Martin with a selection of local varieties

Edible oils

The edible oil industry is dominated by soybean, palm, oil seed rape, sunflower, peanut, palm kernel and olive oils. Yet, as our tastes diversify and our lifestyles change, other oils are becoming more prevalent in the marketplace. From linseed oil to the oil obtained from apricot kernels, whether high in allegedly healthier polyunsaturated fats or low in less desirable trans fatty acids, edible oils help to lubricate global economics and our well-being.

Sunflower oil

Sunflowers (*Helianthus annuus*) provide the fourth most important edible oil in the world. A single hectare of sunflowers can yield over 1,000 litres of oil. Currently the world's sunflowers occupy an area slightly under the size of the UK.

First cultivated about 2,000 years ago in North America, sunflowers were grown for a wide range of uses, including food and as a source of dyes used in textiles, on pottery and as body paint. Yet not for another 3,000 years did the sunflower start to be grown for its edible oil. Sunflower plants were introduced in southern Russia in the eighteenth century, but it was not until oily foods were banned by the Russian Orthodox Church that mass cultivation began, the sunflower not being on the Church's list of prohibited oils. Today the sunflower, possibly the only major domesticated food crop to have originated in North America, remains Russia's most important oil crop.

Across the other side of the globe Argentina was starved of its essential supply of olive oil during the Spanish Civil War in the 1930s. As a

result Argentina started sunflower oil production and is now one of the leaders of the edible oil industry. France, Spain and Italy are the biggest producers in Europe. To date the UK's relatively cool climate limits production.

Olive oil

From the time the dove was supposed to have brought Noah his olive branch over ten thousand years ago, man and the olive (*Olea europaea*) have gone hand in hand. Today there are over seven hundred different varieties of olive, around 10 million hectares of olive groves in the world (equivalent to an area half the size of the UK), and we consume over 2 million tonnes of olive oil a year. On average one olive will produce one drop of oil. Most of the world's olive trees and most of the consumption of their products occur in the Mediterranean regions. Our UK consumption of about 0.5 litres a year per head is dwarfed by the Greeks, who consume over twenty-two litres.

The olive tree grows naturally between southern Africa and the eastern Mediterranean basin, and was probably first cultivated in the area that is now Syria and Palestine. Howard Carter discovered olive twigs in the tomb of Tutankhamun (1352–1325 BC). Also unearthed was a twelfth-century BC papyrus from Pharaoh Rameses III giving the olive groves of Heliopolis to the god Ra. Translated it reads, 'From these trees the purest oil can be extracted to keep the lamps of your sanctuary burning.'

The Minoans introduced the Greeks and the Romans to the olive, and the Greeks capitalized on this new and wonderful source of oil, entering full commercial production. Homer described olive oil as 'liquid gold', and several hundred years later Aristotle wrote about the science of oil production. But it was the Romans who invented mechanical oil extraction and improved storage. The Arabs entered olive oil production, passing their knowledge to the Spanish at the conquest.

Nets are positioned to catch the olives during the harvest in Calabria, Italy

Originally olive oil lit lamps and anointed kings, rather than dressing salads and frying onions. The tree was deemed sacred, its branches symbolizing peace, wisdom and victory, its trunk fertility and prosperity, and its oil the divine essence.

Olives are still picked by hand. Traditionally granite stones are used to grind the olives into a paste, which is then laid between mats and pressed in a multi-layered press to squeeze out the oil. Using this method, different stages in the pressing produce three different qualities of oil: flowers oil, extra virgin and virgin.

The oil contains high levels of valuable oleic acid, a monounsaturated fat, and other essential fatty acids in an optimum ratio, similar to those of maternal milk. As well as emulsifying fats for digestion, the oil is highly digestible, activates the liver's functions, helps to stimulate bile production, reputedly lowers blood cholesterol, helps to absorb the liposoluble vitamins A, D, E and K, and is a strong antioxidant.

The increasing demand for olive oil has led to a dramatic increase in the use of pesticides, which has led to significant localized health and environmental problems. Every year around 34 tonnes of parathion-methyl is used on olive trees to control their pests. The European Union is now working with producers across Mediterranean countries to lower this chemical input, and in some areas integrated pest management has reduced pesticide applications by up to 90 per cent.

Palm oil

Many of our favourite foods, including ice cream, chocolate and crisps, have palm oil as an ingredient. Ninety per cent of the world's palm oil is used for edible purposes. Non-food uses include soaps, shampoo, lipstick and, more recently, engine oil. Oil palms are the most important oil-producing plants of the tropics; fast growing, they yield a crop within five years. As our demand increases, so does the march into virgin land.

An olive grove in the Bcharre Valley, Lebanon

111

Palm oil production is threatening the rainforests as more and more land is being cleared for plantations. Rapid and dramatic changes are needed in the industry in order to stop the devastation that this popular commodity is causing.

Africa uses what it grows, while the vast plantations of South-east Asia supply the world. Processing the oil also brings its problems: tonne for tonne the oxygen-depleting potential of palm oil mill effluent is a hundred times that of domestic sewage.

Initiatives are being developed to reduce the problems. A lot of research has gone into reducing pesticide levels and cleaning waterways. There is also a movement worldwide to encourage the planting of oil palms on degraded land rather than clearing primary rainforest. The largest Swiss supermarket, Migros, which has a strong commitment to high standards of environmental and social management, is demanding that its palm oil is bought from plantations that are managed in a reasonably sustainable way.

The oil palm is second only to the soybean in terms of world use as a vegetable oil. Labelling schemes are needed to identify sustainably produced palm oil. The UK's Forestry Stewardship Council has begun certifying oil palm plantations, and general guidelines for sustainable management have been set by both non-governmental organizations and several large buyers such as Unilever. The World Wildlife Fund has been lobbying financial institutions to cease funding palm oil plantations that destroy natural forests, with mixed success. One of the biggest companies in oil palm plantations and food processing has taken another look at what local people have been using for oils and fats, and 'found' a tropical tree, Allanblackia (*Allanblackia stuhlmannii, A. floribunda*) which could be harvested on a village level in the humid tropics of Africa. This brings back a human scale and possibilities of retaining biodiversity – in short a sustainable future – as an alternative to an endless monoculture of oil palm.

Oil palm plantation at Douala, south-west Cameroon

New alternatives

Around three hundred different plant species produce edible oils. Fuelled by our demand, the last decade has seen an increase in the number of alternative edible oils in our shops. Linseed oil, unlike many other edible oils, contains high amounts of alpha linolenic acid (ALA), one in a group of compounds called omega 3 essential fatty acids, which may help to prevent heart disease, high blood pressure and arthritis. Insufficient quantities of omega 3 in diets are thought to be a major contributory factor in the rise of inflammatory disorders. Hemp oil, which has a nutty flavour, contains high concentrations of polyunsaturated fats and is regarded as one of the healthiest oils on the market.

Safflower oil, extracted from the thistle-like plant *Carthamus tinctorius*, is flavourless and colourless, and contains high levels of polyunsaturated fats. Almond oil is rich in vitamins A and E; avocado oil is especially good for high-heat cooking, and coconut oil is high in saturated fats. Globally we produce over 700 tonnes of peppermint oil, mostly for use as flavouring in foodstuffs. Cottonseed oil is becoming increasingly used in blended vegetable oil. Grapeseed oil, a by-product of the wine industry, is another good oil for cooking; hazelnut oil has a roasted flavour that goes well with fish; and mustard oil, with its spicy flavour, is widely used in Indian cuisine. Other more unusual oils include those from poppy seed, pine nut, pumpkin, rice bran, tea, walnut and wheat germ.

Linseed fields in South Gloucestershire

Tea

Originally taken as a medicine and ceremonial drink, tea (*Camellia sinensis*) went on to play a significant role in world trade, linking East and West. Second only to water, tea is now the most popular drink in the world. The British are amongst the world's biggest consumers, drinking one-fifth of the world's tea annually – five times more than the rest of Europe put together.

The Chinese have grown tea for over two thousand years, first using it to treat abscesses and tumours, chest inflammations and bladder ailments. They also noticed that it quenched the thirst and kept them awake. Tea drinking reached Europe in the mid-seventeenth century. China tea was the only tea known to Westerners until the late eighteenth century, when the British discovered tea growing wild in the Assam hills of northern India. The Indian tea industry burgeoned in the mid-nineteenth century, using seeds and expertise imported from China, and now exports 200,000 tonnes a year.

Production

Today tea is grown in around forty-five countries in the subtropics and the mountainous regions of the tropics, from sea level to over 2,000 metres. Most tea is grown at fairly high altitudes in a cool, moist mountain climate. The tender evergreen plants flourish in deep, rich soils, even temperatures, high humidity and with at least 1.3 metres of rain a year.

Most tea bushes are pruned into a fan shape with a flat-topped 'plucking table' at a comfortable height. This enables the pickers to pluck two very tender leaves and an unopened bud, known as the 'tips' – as in PG Tips. Experienced pickers, generally women, collect up to 35 kilograms of tea a day, producing 9 kilograms of processed black tea. In some countries tea is harvested mechanically, which produces higher quantities but the tea is of a lower quality.

There are about three thousand different types of teas, their qualities determined by a combination of the type of bush, the region the tea comes from, the size and age of the leaf picked, the processing method and the grade and size of the tea leaf after rolling. Tea cultivation stretches from Georgia in the former USSR to northern Argentina. Asia produces about 79 per cent of the world's tea, with India providing 30 per cent of this. Other major producers include China, Sri Lanka, Indonesia, Thailand, Turkey, Georgia, Kenya, Malawi, Tanzania and Mozambique.

Over-production is currently 2 per cent, enough to keep prices consistently low – better news for consumers than producers.

A new approach

An increase in consumer interest in the ethical sourcing of tea and its production methods has led to the establishment of the Tea Sourcing Partnership (TSP) in Britain. Seventy-five per cent of British tea is bought through the scheme, benefiting twenty-two million workers worldwide. The tea is sourced from estates that look after their workers, providing acceptable standards of education, medical care, housing, and health and safety. The TSP has local staff in every country auditing over twelve hundred estates, talking to both workers and suppliers.

Clipper Teas are one of the UK tea industry's major Fairtrade organizations. They source their tea from independent organizations, manufacturers and retailers who have good working conditions and do not use child labour. They place particular emphasis on organic cultivation and better trading relations with the developing world. All packaging is non-chlorine bleached, from managed, sustained forests and entirely bio-degradable. One difference between the TSP and Fairtrade tea is that in the latter there is a stronger focus on cutting out the middlemen and getting the payments for the tea back to the growers.

Tea harvesting in Vietnam

Cherry picking

Coffee cherries, which ripen all year round, used to be predominantly hand picked. The move towards mechanization may keep production costs down but could bring other problems: entire branches bearing ripe and unripe cherries are stripped, affecting the taste, and any that are dropped are breeding grounds for the coffee cherry borer, which will quickly spread to nearby coffee plants.

Coffee

From the highlands of Ethiopia to the parlours of London society, coffee (*Coffea* spp.) has always been more than just a mere drink. It is an integral part of many cultures, whether as part of a religious ritual or as a catalyst for political debate. Lloyds of London, the *Tatler* and the Royal Society all started life in coffee houses. Every year 400 billion cups are drunk and the multi-billion-dollar trade, which makes it one of the most valuable tropical products on the world market, supports 25 million people directly, another 100 million indirectly and even entire countries. Eighty per cent of the area dedicated to coffee production globally is planted in areas of former or current rainforest. It is grown in thirteen of the world's twenty-five biodiversity hotspots (see page 45).

The trade

Brazil, Vietnam and Colombia produce over half the world's coffee, while the USA imports the most, though per capita the Scandinavians are the highest consumers, drinking nearly three times as much as Americans and five times as much as the British.

Coffee is sold primarily through the futures markets in New York and London. New York handles the milder-flavoured, more expensive Arabica beans and London the stronger, cheaper Robusta. The chain from producer to consumer is usually long, each link taking a share of the profits. Much of the value of coffee comes from the processing, most of which is done outside the producing countries. For countries that rely heavily on coffee for their national income changes in coffee prices can affect not just individual farmers but the stability and economic development of an entire nation.

Coffee producers have been facing particularly hard times in recent years as world prices have plummeted. Farmers are now getting less, in real terms, than they were a hundred years ago. This has led to their trying to increase their productivity and reduce costs. Newcomers to the coffee game such as Vietnam and Indonesia have gone for large-scale intensive farming systems with low production costs.

The future

The problems facing coffee producers are now widely recognized and governments, national coffee associations and organizations are working together with the big multinational roasting companies that buy over half of all coffee, the smaller companies (representing the speciality and niche markets), and the farmers themselves, to find ways of dealing with the issues.

CABI Bioscience, a not-for-profit organization that provides a research and information service to farmers and the related industries of various cash crops, has produced a coffee compendium with input from farmers, scientists, traders, roasters and others involved in the coffee industry. This has a wealth of information that will help farmers, particularly small-scale growers who are often geographically isolated and have limited access to information, to improve their crop quality and be more informed about market prices so that they are not so vulnerable to control by local traders.

Certification schemes have been introduced that pay a premium for sustainably grown coffee, such as the Rainforest Alliance ECO-OK scheme, and the Fairtrade mark (see page 93). The cost of meeting the certification standards and purchasing the stamp of approval can sometimes be prohibitive for small-scale farmers and does not always allow for those who do not yet meet all the criteria. One coffee chain is trying out a points system with a sliding scale of premiums. The only prerequisite is that the coffee is of a certain standard.

Sun or shade?

Sun-grown coffee using cleared forest and large-scale monoculture systems has an impact on the biodiversity of the surrounding areas. Coffee farms using traditional forest shade-grown methods have a significantly higher biodiversity and provide an important stopover for migrating birds. The shade-grown coffee farms and surrounding forests of El Savador provide this vital service for up to five billion migratory birds as they journey from North America to the warm tropics each winter. Eden is acting as an outlet for shade-grown coffee in order to help tell its story.

There are some concerns that providing a financial incentive for shade-grown or bird-friendly coffee will lead to further destruction of natural forests. Not all shade-grown coffee uses natural shade; some rely on crop shade such as cocoa trees that have been planted after forest clearance. Rigorous certification, such as that of the Rainforest Alliance ECO-OK scheme, is essential.

Many of the big roasters are now involved in sustainable farming projects. The USA's coffee industry recently established a volunteer Coffee Corps to provide expert assistance on quality

Ripening coffee cherries

improvement in producer countries. The speciality and so-called niche markets of organic and Fairtrade coffees are on the increase. Over 40 per cent of the US market is now in the speciality sector and while coffee consumption in the UK is falling as a whole, the Fairtrade market is increasing.

Choosing good-quality coffee helps to support the farmers who invest the most in their crops, sending a clear message to the roasting companies that quality is important to their customers. To get quality, farmers need to be paid a fair price that is enough not only to cover their production costs but also to support their families and to invest in future harvests. This helps the farmers and also protects the valuable habitats in which coffee is grown and the biodiversity they support.

The coffee stall – part of Eden's Coffee exhibit

Alcoholic drinks

Beer

Beer is the world's most popular alcoholic drink and is as old as civilization itself. In Europe we make it from barley (*Hordeum* spp.) fermented with yeast. Elsewhere in the world it is also made from maize, millet, rice, rye and sorghum. In 2003 'c/o British Farming' conducted a survey of a thousand people as part of its campaign to help reconnect people with the countryside. Nearly 90 per cent didn't know that barley was the main ingredient of beer.

Brewing began in the Fertile Crescent, where wild barley was harvested twenty-seven thousand years ago. Beer and leavened bread both depend on fermentation, and both may have been discovered simultaneously, perhaps from gruel that fermented with natural yeast.

In the days before water was piped it was suspect, being known to carry dangerous diseases, and people preferred to drink beer instead. Beer was enjoyable, nutritious and safe, even for infants. In the Middle Ages people drank six pints (3.5 litres) a day, but the beer was weaker then.

Today hops (*Humulus lupulus*) are used in beer-making to impart the distinctive bitter taste, though originally they were added as a preservative, to stop the beer going sour. Hops are susceptible to several pests and diseases and often require spraying. Recently a new hop variety has been launched that is suitable for organic production with minimal use of pesticide: 'Boadicea' is a dwarf English female hop that is resistant to damson hop aphid and powdery and downy mildew.

Hop poles in Eden's Beer exhibit

Grape vines

Wild grapes, growing in the warm wooded valleys of the Caucasus mountains, were first cultivated at least six thousand years ago. Yet we would never have learnt to celebrate life and love with wine had the grape not grown yeasts on its skin. When the fruit skin burst, these yeasts turned sugars into alcohol, and wine became the life-blood of ceremony, both sacred and profane.

European wines are made from *Vitis vinifera*, which do not grow outside the Old World. Cuttings of American species taken to Europe brought with them white mildew (*Oidium*). An attempt in 1860 to cure the disease in Europe, by using vine cuttings from eastern America, introduced a far worse pest, *Phylloxera*, which ruins both the crop and the vine. *Phylloxera* spread worldwide, doing about £25 billion worth of damage in today's prices. It was forty years before a solution was perfected by grafting European varieties on to *Phylloxera*-resistant American rootstock. Nearly all commercial vines are now grown in this way. A third wine pathogen came from California in the nineteenth century: downy mildew (*Daktulosphaira vitifoliae*). The copper fungicides that cure it were discovered by accident. A spray was made from grape must fermenting on copper sheets and it was sprayed to stop children scrumping grapes, but it was then noticed that it prevented mildew.

Studies have shown that moderate alcohol consumption may decrease mortality from heart disease by 40 per cent. Red wine is believed to get its extra-beneficial effects from a naturally occurring fungicide, resveratrol, a substance that has been used for years to combat heart disease by Japanese, Chinese and Korean herbal doctors. (Resveratrol is also found in the root of the dreaded Japanese knotweed – perhaps a use for this invasive weed?) Red wine protects coronary arteries by removing the harmful cholesterol that

Grape vines growing near Bingen, Germany...

can settle on artery walls, making the platelets in blood less sticky and so less likely to form clots, and by the antioxidant action of resveratrol that mops up the dangerous 'free radicals' that can cause artery damage and cancer.

Vine futures

In the Bacchus project satellites from the European Space Agency are being used to beam back images of vineyards which can provide vital information about the geology of a wine-growing area. An Israeli company has come up with a new plant-monitoring system that uses extremely fine sensors developed from Soviet space programme technology. The sensors measure plant growth, evaporation, leaf temperature, sap flow, soil temperature, soil moisture, air temperature, humidity, solar radiation and more besides. If the vines require attention, the sensors call the farmer's computer to let him know. The system also allows him to modify

Maenad in Eden vines

his irrigation scheme for precise control of the crop output, making the grapes sweeter by withholding water at certain times of day, for example.

...and in the hotter climate of Rioja, Spain

121

Spices

Spices were once worth more than their weight in gold. Dreams of wealth from spices drove merchant seamen far beyond the edges of their known world to discover America, Brazil and Japan by accident, launching a brutal period of trade and colonial expansion.

Peppercorns made salted meat palatable and were so valuable in the eleventh century that they were counted out one by one. Taxes and rents were paid in the spice – hence the term 'peppercorn rent'. Spices travelled to Europe from the Orient by camel-train along the silk route, or by sailing ship from South China to India and then the Persian Gulf. The Arab spice merchants told tall tales to discourage competition. Marco Polo, a Venetian merchant, revealed the true source of spices as 'Zipangu' (China) and the court of Kublai Khan. This knowledge unleashed five hundred years of struggle between European states.

The history of spice

Spice of life and death The quest for the sea route to the Spice Islands was driven by greed and fear: greed for cargoes of dried fruit, seeds and roots that could make instant fortunes, and fear of death from the plague. Plague first burst upon Europe in 1346, having travelled along the spice and silk road from Central Asia. Within five years it had slain a third of the population of Europe. Spices such as nutmeg were held to be sovereign cures. In 1498, Vasco da Gama reached India. After a two-year voyage that cost the lives of half his crew, he returned to Lisbon, to a hero's welcome, with a cargo of pepper and cinnamon.

Spain sails West The Genoese Columbus promised King Ferdinand and Queen Isabella of Spain that he could outflank the Portuguese and bring them spice riches by a different route. In 1492 he sailed west off the edge of the map, finding Central America by mistake, while the Portuguese sailed east and discovered the Spice Islands, Tidore, the source of cloves, and the Banda Islands. There, and only there, grew the nutmeg, and 10 pounds (4.5 kilograms) of nutmegs cost a penny. In London they were worth six thousand times as much. By the seventeenth century, a pocketful of nutmeg was worth a mansion in Holborn.

The Earth girdled In 1519 Ferdinand Magellan set course for the Banda Islands, funded by Spain. Over 620 miles south of the River Plate he found a storm-racked strait. The ocean beyond was so calm by comparison that he called it the Pacific. Magellan was killed in an inter-tribal squabble in the Philippines. Laden with cloves, nutmeg, cinnamon and mace, the last of Magellan's five ships finally returned to Seville in 1522.

The spice race In 1602 the Dutch East India Company was formed to seize the Spice Islands trade. By 1619 it was the biggest trading corporation in Europe, and the Dutch became the first Europeans to explore Australia, Tasmania and New Zealand. In the seventeenth century Holland reached the zenith of its power as Europe's richest state – mostly because of spice.

The ever-increasing success of the Dutch finally spurred the English into action. In 1600 the British East India Company was chartered by Queen Elizabeth to trade spice. But in 1609 the experienced Dutch commander Peter Verhoef sailed with instructions to take the islands on which grew cloves and nutmeg 'by treaty or by force'. He took this as permission to slaughter any islanders who opposed him. This began a cat-and-mouse struggle for cargoes of nutmeg between the more powerful Dutch presence and visiting English fleets. The nutmeg forests on Run, an outlying island of the Bandas most easily reached by the English, were systematically destroyed and the Dutch decided to corner the clove market by destroying clove production everywhere except on Amboina. The Dutch ruled the spice markets with a rod of iron. If the price of cinnamon fell too low in Amsterdam they burnt it.

In 1665 two English ships regained Run, but it was recaptured by the Dutch and for the second time they destroyed all the nutmeg trees.

Spices remain an integral part of almost every cuisine

The spice boat – centrepiece of Eden's Spice exhibit

This so angered the Duke of York that he ordered vessels across the Atlantic to seize the Dutch island of Manhattan. The small farming and trading town of New Amsterdam was renamed New York. Three years later, at the Treaty of Breda, the English relinquished their claims on Run, the Dutch theirs on New York. A nutmeg isle was swapped for the future 'big apple'.

Spices escape worldwide In 1780, the Dutch and the English fought another war, which was to be ruinously costly to the Dutch East India Company. In 1810 Captain Cole stormed the Dutch fortifications on the Banda Islands and they remained under British control for seven years. Nutmeg seedlings were transported to Ceylon, Singapore and elsewhere and production in the Banda Islands was swamped by the new plantations. The island of Run, once one of the most important destinations, disappeared off the maps of the world.

The French succeeded in transporting clove trees to Mauritius and Reunion in 1770, then reached Zanzibar, which became the principal source of cloves for the market. Today Indonesia is the largest producer and exporter of cloves. Vanilla was taken from Central America to Reunion and Madagascar on the other side of the globe. The British took the ginger plant from India to Jamaica, and the nutmeg to the West Indies. It is now Grenada in the Windward Islands that is known as the 'nutmeg isle', although most of its plantations were destroyed by hurricanes in the summer of 2004 and will take a long time to recover.

All this history just to flavour our food!

Sugar

Sugar cane sticks were first chewed for their sugary sap in New Guinea ten thousand years ago. By the fourteenth century sugar was a European luxury, with consumption around a teaspoon per head per year. Today we consume around 3 kilograms a week each and a greater weight of raw sugar cane is harvested round the world than wheat. Nutritionally we don't need it, but it is a major crop in world trade, is stored during times of political instability or food shortages and supports the economies of many developing countries. Its rise to stardom is based on an appalling history of human exploitation and bitter trade wars.

Sugar cane (*Saccharum officinarum*) is a giant grass that thrives in a warm, moist climate, storing sugar as a sappy pulp in its stalk. Nearly 90 per cent of the weight of the cane is juice, which contains up to 17 per cent sucrose (common sugar) and small amounts of dextrose and fructose.

Sugar cane has been intensively cultivated in the past, causing considerable damage both to the environment and to the workers. However over the last few decades there have been major improvements that have made economic and environmental sense. Sugar extraction from beet (*Beta vulgaris*) started in the eighteenth century and developed in Europe as a result of blockades during the Napoleonic Wars. In 2004, 70 per cent of global sugar production came from cane and 30 per cent from beet.

Sugar cane fields in Brazil

Sugar and slavery

Sugar cane was possibly the first industrial crop and has a long association with slave labour. Slaves were used for sugar production in the Mediterranean at the time of the Crusades and they were also used when the crop spread to the islands off the coast of Africa. It was taken to Hispaniola (now Haiti and the Dominican Republic) by Columbus as a potential cash crop and by the year 1600 sugar production in the subtropical and tropical Americas had become the world's largest and most lucrative industry.

The harsh conditions and an influx of diseases from the Old World soon decimated the local population in the Caribbean, so African slaves were brought in to meet the growing requirement for labour. By the 1650s Caribbean sugar production had become dominant and remained the centre of world production until the 1850s. As a result of the Napoleonic Wars and the acute labour shortage brought about by the British emancipation of slaves in 1833, the West Indian planters felt the effect of competition from countries such as Cuba, Puerto Rico and Brazil, where slave labour was still employed.

Sugar cane today

Sugar cane is now grown in over a hundred tropical and subtropical countries, most of which are underdeveloped. Sugar cane produces the highest unprocessed yield of all the world's

Sugar cane is often harvested by hand

crops at about 600 million tonnes. At least seven million people are employed in the sugar industry and thirty million are directly dependent on sugar industry income. Seventy per cent of sugar is consumed where it is grown and yet one of the most controversial issues regarding sugar production today is its trade.

Almost all sugar producers have some kind of price support and most is sold by bilateral trade agreements at higher than world trade price. Although often perceived as subsidies, trade agreements to developing countries can be a form of aid that reaches farmers more effectively than direct aid payments. The European Union (EU) is a major exporter of sugar from beet but because of historical links to traditional suppliers, imports of sugar cane from the former African, Caribbean and Pacific (ACP) colonies have been protected by trade agreements that enable these countries to compete with developed economies. For countries with economies that rely heavily on sugar sales and are ACP members, this has worked well, but this is not the case for non-ACP countries, whose farmers can suffer great hardship when there is a sudden and unexpected fall in the world price.

Pressure to end this preferential system has come from the World Trade Organization and the EU itself. New rules will mean that preferential prices paid to European sugar beet producers and ACP cane sugar producers will be phased out. Some welcome this as a means of increasing free access to the EU market. Concerns are being expressed by the producer countries, however, that this may drive prices down and make it uneconomic to export to the EU. Some believe that the new rules will benefit only the lowest cost producers and that removing the preferential prices will end what has been seen as a form of aid to the poorest sugar cane workers.

There is concern that reliance on a few low-cost producers could leave much of the world exposed to unpredictable movements in the world market. Developing countries with higher costs may not be able to compete with these lower-cost producers. In some areas there are already signs of unemployment, social unrest, increased urban migration and emigration.

Ways forward include growing something else or finding alternative uses for sugar cane production. Brazil's production has expanded dramatically because of its ability to switch between producing sugar and production of bioethanol for use as vehicle fuel. In Hawaii sugar cane is being grown as a renewable fuel for electricity generation and sugar is a by-product. Meanwhile sugar's role in deteriorating dental health and as a major contributor to obesity – particularly as a hidden ingredient in processed food – is coming under increasing scrutiny.

Cocoa

For almost three thousand years cacao – better known as cocoa – and chocolate have been both worshipped and forbidden. Once enjoyed by the privileged few, chocolate is now the luxury of the masses, a guilty pleasure for some, a live-lihood for others.

Chocolate comes from the beans of the cacao tree (*Theobroma cacao*, theobroma meaning 'food of the gods'). It was in the tropical forests of Central or South America that the first of many Mesoamerican peoples, the Olmec, began harvesting cacao and making a drink with it. The Maya who followed them not only drank it, calling it *xocoatl*, but also used the beans as currency. The Aztecs revered cacao trees, believing them to be of divine origin and a bridge between heaven and Earth. They used both beans and drinks, sometimes called

cacahuatl, in religious ceremonies from marriages to human sacrifices and from harvest festivals to coming-of-age rituals. Montezuma, the legendary Aztec leader, was famous for the amount of frothy cacao drink he consumed, particularly before a visit to his vast harem, which helped to fuel the belief that chocolate was an aphrodisiac.

When explorer Hernando Cortés arrived in Mexico fresh from his exploits in South America, he was welcomed by Aztec nobility, who mistook him for their god Quetzalcoatl. They plied him with cacao drinks served in golden goblets; he overthrew their leadership and conquered the country. When he returned to Spain he took cacao with him. London's first chocolate house opened in 1657. As its popularity increased, the Church began to regard chocolate as a source of greed and evil and attempted to discourage people from drinking it. By the following century the tables had turned and chocolate was being sold by the Quaker-owned companies Fry, Cadbury and Rowntree as an alternative to alcohol, which was believed to be one of the causes of poverty and depriva-tion amongst the working class.

Chocolate didn't appear in solid form until 1847, when Joseph Fry's great-grandson produced the first bar of chocolate, with John Cadbury following on his heels two years later. In Britain £3 billion was spent on chocolate in 2003.

Where does it all come from?

During the late nineteenth century, with demand for chocolate increasing, cacao trees were taken from Central and South America and transplanted in the Côte d'Ivoire and Ghana in West Africa. Today, most of the 3 million tonnes

The large cocoa pods grow from the main branches

of cocoa beans grown every year still come from there. South America, the home of cocoa, provides only a small proportion of the world supply.

It wasn't always this way. In the early 1990s the Brazilian crop was decimated by a fungal disease and Brazilian production has never recovered. Twenty-five per cent of global production is still lost to this disease annually. African cocoa farmers face a similar disease which causes the loss of over a third of the global crop. These diseases are often dealt with by heavy use of toxic and expensive pesticides.

To tackle these problems the industry is working with farmers to give them tools and knowledge to maintain a healthy crop without the need for expensive chemicals or equipment. The Biscuit, Cake, Chocolate and Confectionery Association (BCCCA), whose members include major chocolate companies, is just one of the organizations involved worldwide in trying to encourage sustainable farming practices. Amongst other things they run field schools for farmers in West Africa, looking at agricultural and labour issues, including the use of children in the workforce. This sensitive issue is being addressed by the industry following reports in 2001 that children were being used as forced labour on some farms. As a result the International Cocoa Initiative was established to oversee and sustain efforts to eliminate the worst forms of child labour by creating and managing farmers' groups, educating suppliers and developing a certification process. The issue is a complex one, exacerbated by the number of people involved in the cocoa supply chain.

Cocoa pods are picked and split open by hand. For many cocoa growers the involvement of the whole family, particularly in harvesting the crop, is essential especially when cocoa prices are low and the money they make does not even cover their production costs. As some 80 per cent of cocoa is grown on smallholdings of just a few hectares, it is difficult for buyers of vast quantities of beans to track the origins of a consignment that will have come from many hundreds of individual farms. The work being done to develop low-cost, sustainable methods of farming, and increase yields without increasing costs, together with the concerted efforts of the industry as a whole, shows a real commitment to improving conditions for growers. Scientists are trying to breed disease-resistant varieties of cocoa, which may be the answer in the long term. In the meantime the industry and growers are working hard to find some positive solutions that ensure a continued supply of one of our best-loved indulgences.

A guide in the Humid Tropics Biome showing a freshly opened cocoa pod

Gum and coke

At the Alamo in 1836, General Antonio de Santa Anna introduced America to the habit of chewing gum. Fifty years later Dr John S. Pemberton introduced the world to another product by adding the extracts of the African kola nut to a fizzy drink. Every day half a billion people around the globe consume this drink, and in America many people chew over three hundred sticks of gum a year.

Kola or cola originates from the seeds of two tree species (*Cola acuminate* and *Cola nitida*). The seed is widely chewed across Africa as a stimulant to dispel sleep, thirst and hunger, and is surrounded by cultural significance. The origins of the well-known drink lay in a medicinal flu treatment, a powerful mixture of red wine and cocaine, hence 'coca'. Pemberton replaced the red wine with carbonated water and added cola extract following the 1886 Prohibition Act. Cocaine (*Erythroxylum coca*) was removed from the secret recipe in 1904, but cola remained as a source of natural flavouring and caffeine. As the demand for the drink went global and natural sources could not meet the escalating success of the drink, cola was replaced with a caffeine alternative.

Chewing gum was first made from natural chicle, a latex harvested from wild populations of the sapodilla tree (*Manilkara zapota*) in Central American rainforests. By the 1960s natural chewing gum was largely replaced by cheap and easy-to-manufacture styrene-butadiene rubber, and the chicle industry in Central America collapsed.

Today cola and chewing gum, or at least their synthetic alternatives, remain big business. While new information and communication technologies have shrunk the globe and accelerated our pace of life, globalization continues to change the way we use plants. Following the over-exploitation of some plants to meet growing global demands for products, the replacement of natural products with synthetic substitutes may be one of conservation's key strategies for success.

Cola flowers growing at Eden

Harvesting chicle in Mexico, near the border with Belize

Voices on food

It's 2005. There are around 6.3 billion people in the world. Of these, 2 billion suffer from chronic undernutrition and 18 million die annually from hunger-related diseases – yet we grow more sugar in the world than we do wheat. We're adding 80 million more mouths to feed each year – mostly in countries that are the least capable of providing them with food. There is increased pressure on the land, an increased urban population and potential changes caused by climate change. There are those who say that there would be enough food in the world to feed everyone if it were distributed more evenly. Some research suggests that there are more overweight people on the planet than underweight, but it is not just a matter of the poor starving and the rich having heart attacks. Diet-related diseases are on the up in low- and medium-income countries too.

So what are the underlying drivers to our food issues? Environmental, social or both? Most importantly, what are the choices for the future? Here are a few thoughts from some of the people who are working on food.

First things first
'You cannot build peace on empty stomachs.' John Boyd Orr, the first director-general of the United Nations Food and Agriculture Organization and Nobel Peace Prize winner

Past predictions
'The battle to feed all of humanity is over. In the 1970s and 1980s hundreds of millions of people will starve to death in spite of any crash programs embarked upon now.'

Paul Erlich, *The Population Bomb*, 1968

Breeding for the twenty-first century
'There is no magic in high-yielding varieties alone, we've got to have plants that have built-in resistance to diseases and pests and that have improved nutritive value ... there is no new land to be brought into production. All food that is produced must come from the land already in production.'

Norman E. Borlaug, speaking to the Auburn University College of Agriculture, Alabama, USA at the beginning of the twenty-first century.

Borlaug, father of the 'Green Revolution', was awarded the 1970 Nobel Peace Prize for developing high-yield, disease-resistant wheat strains and introducing those plants, along with improved farming practices, to hunger-plagued Third World countries, saving millions worldwide from starvation in the 1960s. In the early twenty-first century, at ninety, he still travels the world seeking to improve production of wheat, corn, cassava and other staples.

Root causes

'In the industrialized countries of the northern hemisphere, surplus production is the norm and farmers are paid not to farm some land (to "set aside" the land) in order to reduce food output and surpluses. The main cause of hunger is poverty. In the 1980s, Ethiopia was a net exporter of grain despite famine among its own population. Nearly 80 per cent of malnourished children in the southern hemisphere live in countries that have food surpluses. Where hunger exists, what is often lacking is not food but access to it – either having the money to buy it or the land to grow it.'

Myth and Reality. Organic vs. non-organic: The facts (joint report by the Soil Association and Sustain, 2001)

Listen to the people who live off the land

'A sustainable solution to famine also means a proper valuing of traditional knowledge and skills, and encouraging the poorest families to feed themselves by planting traditional multiple crops in a mixture. It is women and small farmers working with biodiversity who are the primary food producers in the Third World and, contrary to the dominant assumption, their biodiversity-based small farm systems are more productive than industrial monocultures.'

Vandana Shiva, Reith Lecture, 2000

Sustainable agriculture

'Sustainable agricultural management can contribute significantly to both net carbon sequestration and to increased food production, as well as making a significant impact on rural people's livelihoods. In 208 projects analysed in fifty-two countries, average per-hectare food production increased by 73 per cent and there were additional beneficial side effects though improvements in water tables, reduced soil erosion and increased agro-biodiversity.'

Professor Jules Pretty, Director, Centre for Environment and Society, University of Essex

Local food economies

'In an age of dwindling oil supplies and climate change, it is nothing short of criminal that nations around the world routinely export and import identical products (including fresh milk and live animals), often in almost identical quantities. We urgently need to shift economic policies away from such senseless trade towards support for diversified, local food economies. This does not mean eliminating all trade; rather, our goal should be to meet our basic needs from as close to home as possible.

Local food economies not only help to reduce the waste and pollution of packaging, processing and transportation, but encourage more sustainable, organic means of production. What's more, farmers get a better price for their products, while consumers pay less for fresh, healthy food.'

Helena Norberg-Hodge, Director of the International Society for Ecology and Culture

Buy local, buy seasonal

'It can be argued that air-freighted green beans from East Africa use no more energy than out-of-season growing of green vegetables in heated glasshouses in northern Europe. Both represent an unsustainable use of finite fossil fuels ... I am not suggesting that we should never eat imported or out-of-season food, only that if we understood the impact our choices made on other parts of our lives, we might make slightly different choices.'

Felicity Lawrence, *Not on the Label*, Penguin, 2004

Food miles

'Transporting food long distances is energy ineffi-cient. One imported basket of food could release as much carbon dioxide into the atmosphere as an average four-bedroom household does through cooking for eight months.'

Lawrence Woodward and Andy Jones, *Eating Oil*, Elm Farm Research Centre, 2002

Food for energy

It takes energy to make the food that gives us energy. There is an enormous amount of energy leakage in the food production system. The more processed the food, the greater the energy investment; the greater the energy investment, the greater the production of pollutants. On average the modern production and distribution system expends 10–15 calories of energy for every calorie of food energy produced.

Meat or grain?

A large proportion of the world's staples is currently fed to animals. In the EU, 75 per cent of agricultural land is used for growing fodder. A meat-based diet requires seven times more land than a plant-based diet, and in the developing world there is a move away from vegetarian to meat-based diets, thus compounding the problem of supply. Cutting down on our meat consumption could increase food supplies for all. Meat is important, however, where animals are produced by extensive grazing of lands that cannot produce crops, such as upland hill farms in the UK and in many semi-arid regions in the world.

Integrated policies

'Challenges cannot be met in a piecemeal fashion. There has to be a new vision ... links across policy areas ... continuity in thinking ... from the way our food is produced to the management of consump-tion and the healthiness of foodstuffs ... a new conception of health – linking human and ecological health – has to be at the heart of a new policy vision.'

Tim Lang, Professor of Food Policy, City University, London

134

Informed choices

'People are increasingly worried about their own health, as they choose between different food products, but not so much about the health of the environment or those involved in producing the food. At the same time, they demand more action from the Government on pollution, and health and safety issues. If the Government responds by increasing regulation, food businesses in a global marketplace are tempted to go to suppliers elsewhere in the world, where standards may well be less than people would like. By buying products, people are effectively endorsing the standards applied by those who supply them, which most retailers don't make clear.

Without better information about the social and environmental impacts of growing, processing and transporting what's on the shelf, consumers can't even start to take better-informed decisions. Yet, sustainable development depends on better-informed decisions, or people can't start to consume more wisely. If we don't even know the impact of our consumption decisions, we stand no chance of handing on a world in better condition to the world's children and grandchildren.'

Richard Wakeford, Head of the Scottish Executive Environment and Rural Affairs Department, former Chief Executive of the Countryside Agency and member of the UK Sustainable Development Commission

Food for thought

The last century saw a revolution in agriculture more profound than any since the very first steps of settled farming were taken. Industrial and scientific developments have made it possible for those who have the right sort of resources to expand vastly the scale of production, to reduce the risk of crop failure and extend cropping on to land that previously was of only marginal productivity.

Delving into scientific agricultural textbooks of the time, it is striking that everyone was conceiving of their work as focused on increasing yield, but paradoxically this was probably one of the least significant achievements. There are plenty of documented examples of smallholder mixed farming systems that produce as much, or more, yield per area than agri-industrial farming. So what has the modern agricultural age really brought us?

Traditional mixed farming relied on the diversity of crops and production systems to ensure that even in bad seasons enough food was produced. Modern industrial farming uses a range of techniques to ensure that, whatever the variation in season and land quality (within reason), a reliable and uniform single crop is

produced, with increasing precision about the timing of harvest. This in turn allows the development of large-scale mechanized systems where the costs of production fall so low that they can more than compensate for transport costs of taking the produce long distances.

The greatest achievement of the Agricultural Revolution has been the huge reduction in the number of people needed to produce food. Today one person can produce the volume of food that once needed hundreds of people working the land. This almost unbelievable achievement has in turn allowed the shift of the majority of the population to cities, and led to major social change in the countryside.

The reliability and uniformity of supply, linked to a transport system that allows food to become globally sourced and thus free from seasonality, has also bolstered the growth of food-processing industries, so that the products we see in supermarkets are increasingly diverse and packaged in novel ways.

The social impact of these changes is almost too profound to think about – we can hardly picture a world where these shifts have not happened. However, the paradoxes as far as agriculture itself is concerned are all too evident.

For example, every 'advance' in agriculture that farmers have taken on board has meant that more and more farmers disappear from the land. To be a successful farmer increasingly relies on having access to major capital to invest. As we gain in richness of foods supplied to us, we begin to value these foods, and the production systems, less and less. Our understanding of, and political support for, farmers and farming systems also erode. Do we also lose something deeper, at a cultural or spiritual level, if we become so divorced from the land and our understanding of our place in the natural world?

On an international level as we see radical advances in food security and the ease of

Rice fields in Madagascar

transporting it, the problems of starvation and poverty in developing countries become ever more frustrating. Is the way forward to industrialize the agriculture of these countries so that they can compete, or is the move to global production and trade keeping them in a poverty trap?

There are also environmental impacts of this new system. The spiralling use of pesticides, energy used to carry foods to places that could have grown them anyway, pollution, waste and erosion of both soil and crop diversity inevitably raises worries that the advances we have gained are built on sand, and that our new-found food security is a short-term blessing.

So we stand today in a world of rapidly polarizing opinions about the way forward. Is the continued industrialization of farming the best or the worst idea we can have? Are the alternatives realistic options for feeding the global population or just luxuries only open to nations that have already enough wealth to buy from the world market when they need to? Does an urbanized and industrialized society need to retain some connection with land and nature to remain sane and civilized?

Health

We live in an age obsessed by health. The pharmaceutical industry panders to both real and imagined need and is worth many billions of dollars a year. Many scourges have been conquered, but the major diseases still have a hold on us and on our imaginations: among them cancers of many descriptions, AIDS and diabetes. None has a certain cure – yet. Pandemics and epidemics stalk the pages of our newspapers and we wonder whether another plague lies in wait for us just around the corner.

Paradoxically some social problems result from the success, rather than the absence, of health provision. There are challenges resulting from the demand for natural medicines, from the moral choices to be made in the provision of expensive healthcare, from equity in global health, from world population growth and comparative life spans as well as from the social and economic demands of an ageing society in the developed world. Gradually there is a recognition that scientific and medical research has tended to focus on 'illness' and 'cure' rather than 'health' and the maintenance of 'well-being'. Driven by escalating health costs, the question of what helps individuals and societies remain healthy is forcing a fundamental re-evaluation of our lifestyles and environments.

Health is a complex matter. A mechanistic view of the world is often advanced by the life sciences and pharmaceutical companies, which would like us to see every failure of health as curable. This view has been supported by advances in the understanding of genetics, leading some commentators to believe that our genes are like car parts that can be tweaked to rid us of imperfection. Despite these views, a holistic approach to medicine, once the preserve of 'alternative' practitioners in developed countries, is now becoming firmly embedded in the mainstream. The 'nature versus nurture' debates that preoccupied the Victorians are still with us as science learns more and more about genetic controls and triggers and also about how intangible factors such as our minds and our environments influence our well-being. The need to understand what role environment and personal choice play in shaping our development is therefore crucial.

This chapter approaches the question of health and well-being from a range of perspectives. We begin with an overview of the direct contribution that medicinal plants can make and the issues that arise from their exploitation. We also look at those plants we use to enhance quality of life, such as perfumes, and those that give pleasure while undermining health, such as tobacco. We finish with an overview of what makes a healthy environment and a healthy planet in the broadest sense.

Plant cures

The story of the search for cures is fascinating and complex. Most of all it is inspirational, blending an exploration of the natural world with the painstaking discipline of science. To tell the story we need to look at not only the plants but also the people. What it is that makes a human work, what fuels do we need to operate, what goes wrong with us, what drives the search for a cure and how does the exploration for a remedy begin? Answering these questions is detective work of the highest quality.

The twist is that underlying this tale of discovery are some of the most difficult issues of our times: the patenting of life, intellectual property rights (that is, ownership of ideas themselves), equity and biopiracy. In the public domain the behaviour of 'Big Pharma' – pharmaceutical companies that plunder the biodiversity and cultural knowledge of poor communities and offer them drugs and medical systems beyond their reach – has become shorthand for the worst examples of corporate greed and exploitation, yet paradoxically the manufacture of many pharmaceuticals is often more sustainable than the wild collection of their herbal equivalents.

Every community in the world once had its own largely plant-based pharmacopoeia. Before the advent of 'modern' medicine that was all there was, and for many communities it remains all that they can afford. Many of these traditions

Medicinal plants play a part in every culture

remain intact, most famously the Ayurvedic tradition, while others, such as treatments using essential oils, have been adapted to the modern world. Historical records from Sumer, Babylon, Egypt, Persia, China, Greece and Rome show a long use of plant-based medicine. Recent excavations in the middens at a monastery in northern England have demonstrated the huge breadth of treatments that were provided by the monks against a wide range of ailments. Witch doctors, witches, shamans and medicine men have been conducting tests over millennia. Today some drug companies see medicinal use of plants as fertile ground for prospecting.

It is estimated that only 5 per cent of the world's plant species have had the full spectrum of their pharmaceutical potential tested in laboratories. The contribution of willow (aspirin), foxglove (digoxin), opium poppies

Foxglove – source of the heart drug digoxin

(heroin, codeine, morphine) and *Cinchona* (quinine) are relatively well known, even though the need to standardize doses and avoid side effects from secondary chemicals means that these days we use purified or synthesized drugs rather than the herbs themselves.

In recent years high-profile treatments for cancer have been extracted from the Madagascar periwinkle (*Catharanthus roseus*) and Pacific yew (*Taxus brevifolia*), emphasizing, if such emphasis were needed, that the plant kingdom is a vital resource for our future. As vital for our future is the need to protect and preserve this resource.

Eden's medicinal trail

There are hundreds of medicinal plants at Eden, representing many different traditions of medicine from around the world.

The zigzag path into the pit is lined with English yew (*Taxus baccata*). Toxic to livestock (and to humans if the seeds are ingested), this becomes a vital pharmaceutical drug when the leaves are processed into taxol or taxoterre. One of the successes of the American National Cancer

Echinacea – good for the immune system

Program of the 1950s and '60s, yew produces drugs for ovarian, uterine and breast cancers.

Tall Maidenhair trees (*Ginkgo biloba*) show the plant's typical maidenhair fern-like leaf, which is now one of the most popular herbal medicines for memory loss and circulatory problems, traded into the German medicinal plant markets from plantations in China where it is sustainably harvested from field-grown plants maintained as hedges.

In the Herbal and Pharmaceutical Crops exhibit are row crops of St John's Wort (*Hypericum perforatum*), traditionally used as a wound herb but now grown commercially as a herbal remedy for mild depression. Adjacent are rows of pharmaceutical opium poppy (*Papaver somniferum*), grown for the commercial extraction of morphine in Tasmania (and recently in Wiltshire and Hampshire), where it is harvested

from the dried poppy straw. *Echinacea* (in the forms *E. purpurea* and *E. pallida*) are extremely colourful in July and August. This remedy from the Amerindian tradition is used now as an immune system stimulant and, with *Hypericum*, is a top herbal seller.

In the Blue Border grows the wooly foxglove (*Digitalis lanata*), cultivated for the extraction of the heart drug digoxin. In the Herb Garden is feverfew (*Tanacetum parthenium*), which is a herbal remedy for migraine, eaten as a fresh leaf in sandwiches, though not effective for every sufferer.

In the Humid Tropics Biome are various *Cinchona* spp. which provide one of the most important historic drugs for malaria, quinine. Known as Jesuit's bark, the bark of this Andean tree, used by missionaries, famously failed to save the life of Oliver Cromwell, who refused to

Ginkgo biloba – for memory loss and circulatory problems

Pomegranate – used by some to treat worms and diarrhoea

take any remedy favoured by Catholics. Adjacent to the Malaysian House grow several herbs used in Indian Ayurvedic medicine, particularly ashwagandha (*Withania somnifera*), a sedative belonging to the tomato family, and holy basil (*Ocimum tenuiflorum*), which is a pot herb found in nearly every southern Indian backyard, along with the vegetable okra (*Abelmoschus esculentus*), used to calm dysentery. Lemon grass (*Cymbopogon citratus*), used as an insect repellent and to increase appetite, shows how much of Ayurvedic medicine merges the culinary with the healing – your food is your medicine – as does sesame (*Sesamum indicum*), used as a cooking oil but also in Ayurvedic massage mixed with other medicinal herbs. In the temporary vegetable displays, yam vines (*Dioscorea* spp.) twine their way up rapidly in summer. Their tubers were the original source of the contraceptive and topical steroids which have changed the lives of women across the world; and in the Pharmaceutical Crops display is the Madagascar periwinkle (*Catharanthus roseus*), which has saved the lives of thousands of children with leukaemia and those of many others with Hodgkin's disease and other cancers.

In the Warm Temperate Biome is the olive (*Olea europaea*), at the heart of the healthy Mediterranean diet – and also used in the Bach Flower system as a remedy for mental prostration. Spanish sweet chestnut (*Castanea sativa*) is present as handrails in the Biome. Its medicinal use, appropriately, is as a Bach flower remedy for exhaustion.

The perfume of this Biome includes the well-known waft of cistus gum from *Cistus creticus* and *C. ladanifer*, used as a herbal remedy for throat and lung congestion. Here you can also see the pomegranate (*Punica granatum*), the bark of which has been used in Ayurveda for centuries to treat worms and the fruit (which features in the crest of the Royal College of Physicians) for diarrhoea.

In the South African Cape displays the visitor is often assailed by the smell of various species of buchu. These *Agathosma* species are widely used as herbal remedies for arthritis and their oils as urinary antiseptics and diuretics. Among the Orchard Fruit display in the month of May you will see the carrot-relative bishop's-weed (*Ammi majus*), with white flowers. This plant is the source of a psoralen compound which is now synthesized to produce a pharmaceutical remedy for psoriasis in patients who take it orally and are then exposed to ultra-violet light. The plant is often seen in florists' shops as a cut flower.

Eden's Olive exhibit

Wild harvest

It is thought that about twenty-five thousand different plant species are used for medicinal purposes, most of them collected from the wild. The question of their conservation and trade (and wild harvesting in particular) in every country provides a useful prism through which to look at issues of biodiversity.

The conservation of medicinal plants has come into focus only in the past fifteen years. In the past the media has focused more on animal parts used in medicine, such subjects as poaching and the breaking of trade regulations making compelling headlines. However, to people directly dependent on herbs as a local resource, scarcity and extinction caused by over-collection are a real threat. The issue is made worse by the fact that it is often the whole plant that is destroyed, even if only parts, such as bark or roots, are needed.

In Britain our national medicinal heritage is looked after, at the genetic level, by the Millennium Seed Bank at the Royal Botanic Gardens, Kew, based at Wakehurst Place in West Sussex. Kew has undertaken to conserve all our (rather limited) native flora. Ethnobotany in the UK, once a discipline based on 'other people's floras', has enjoyed a boost with the publication of Richard Mabey's *Flora Britannica*, the establishment of courses at the University of Kent at Canterbury, and an organization (Ethnomedica) dedicated to preserving the oral history of 'remembered remedies' in the UK. Various botanic gardens, especially the Chelsea Physic Garden, display the biodiversity of medicinal species.

There is, however, another aspect to conservation in Britain: the additional strain put on resources overseas by the importation of herbs. Most herbs coming into Britain enter by way of the huge wholesale markets in Germany. In the late 1990s a groundbreaking study showed that of 1,560 herbal products imported into Germany, 70–90 per cent were primarily wild

harvested, and that only 50–100 products were produced from cultivated plant species.

The catalogue of one of the few British commercial herb suppliers who list the source of supply showed that 62 per cent of their products came from a cultivated source, about 7.5 per cent were 'wild crafted' (the definition includes an element of sustainability) and just over 30 per

An African herb market

Medicinal herbs on sale in China

cent were wild collected, no information being available on sustainability. Species currently of concern because of wild harvesting in Europe include: pheasant's-eye (*Adonis annua*), bearberry (*Arctostaphylos uva-ursi*), arnica (*Arnica montana*), Iceland moss (*Cetraria islandica*), sundew (*Drosera* spp., especially *D. rotundifolia*, *D. anglica* and *D. intermedia*), yellow gentian (*Gentiana lutea*), liquorice (*Glycyrrhiza glabra*), bogbean (*Menyanthes trifoliata*), oregano (*Origanum* spp.), butcher's broom (*Ruscus aculeatus*) and thyme (*Thymus* spp.).

Asking suppliers for the origin of their products can stimulate awareness of the sustainability issue and add to the pressure for certification schemes to show that products have been sustainably produced, thereby enabling consumers to buy responsibly.

The world picture shows that herbal products are normally gathered or wild crafted with respect for the environment by practising herbalists from their own areas. Herbalists are often the first people to warn that a species is becoming rare. There is some evidence that it is in the development of market trading in herbal products – rather than the collection for

immediate use – that sustainability awareness breaks down. For example, the South African muti markets in Durban and Johannesburg frequently sell species known to be endangered. As a result, every botanic garden in South Africa is now developing display gardens to raise awareness of each region's medicinal flora. Durban's Silver Glen nursery has for many years trained healers to grow their own supplies.

The greatest conservation awareness occurs in the highly biodiverse tropical areas. The Indian government has done more than any other to widen the focus of international trade regulation to include plants as well as animals. There is now international legislation that bans trade in certain species and restricts, by licensing, the quantity of trade in many others including such well-known species as golden seal (*Hydrastis canadensis*) and American ginseng (*Panax quinquefolius*). Countries like India and China have huge internal markets in herbal products. They are often advanced in their research on quality, safety and efficacy; in programmes to conserve germ plasm; and in the development of procedures for nursery production and micropropagation, all of which relieve pressure on the wild (see page 69).

Following the Convention on Biological Diversity in 1992, more and more countries are committed to developing inventories and strategies for preserving their 'own' biodiversity, including its medicinal elements. In one way this is a rationalization of effort; in another it is a 'new nationalism' where natural resources are concerned. So the exploration of 'their' floras by, for example, pharmaceutical companies, is now being governed by new protocols about sharing profits.

In 1998 an International Conference on Medicinal Plants in Bangalore highlighted increasing concern about the rights of traditional peoples. In many countries it is the poor who collect medicinal plants from the wild and there is a delicate balance to be achieved between protecting their incomes and protecting the plants in the wild.

Farming and 'pharming'

Plants are 'turned' into pharmaceutical drugs in a number of ways using three principal routes: farming and extraction of the relevant ingredient, synthesis and a combination of the two.

The pharmaceutical company Glaxo-SmithKline, for example, farms opium poppy (*Papaver somniferum*) in Tasmania, combine-harvests it like wheat, and chemically extracts morphine, papaverine and, subsequently, codeine. Vincristine and vinblastine, two vital oncology drugs used for childhood leukaemias, Hodgkin's disease and many other cancers, are farmed by Eli Lilley in Texas from plantations of the Madagascar periwinkle (*Catharanthus roseus*) (and increasingly in Africa as the drug is now off-patent). The wooly foxglove (*Digitalis lanata*) is farmed for the heart drug digoxin in the Netherlands. Camptothecin, a relatively new oncology drug for colo-rectal and intractable throat and neck cancers, is farmed in China from plantations of the tree *Camptotheca acuminata*. The plants are grown on farms rather than the drug being synthesized because it is cheaper or because the plants' compounds are difficult or impossible to synthesize – as with *Catharanthus*.

In the synthesis route chemists identify an active molecule by screening natural materials, or from ethnobotanical leads or botanical literature trawls, and then synthesize it, often from petrochemicals. Nature is thus used as the chemical template – which is then copied. Examples of synthesized drugs are ephedrine (copied from *Ephedra* spp.), hyoscine (copied from many plants of the Nightshade family

From this store in Ecuador, medicinal herbs are shipped around the world

including mandrake [*Mandragora officinarum*], deadly nightshade [*Atropa belladonna*] and henbane [*Hyoscyamus* spp.]), atropine (copied from deadly nightshade) and aspirin (copied from willow bark [*Salix* spp.] and meadowsweet [*Filipendula ulmaria*]). Synthesis is often important in safeguarding species that would otherwise be over-collected from the wild if they are difficult to cultivate or slow to produce the quantity required.

The third route is a combination of the two above. A plant is cultivated and a precursor chemical is extracted which synthetic chemists then use to manufacture a safer or more complex final product. Examples are etoposide, a drug for lung and testicular cancers, manufactured from an extract of the American mayapple (*Podophyllum peltatum*). Likewise the various taxol drugs for ovarian, uterine and breast cancers are now manufactured from baccatin, a precursor extracted from sustainably harvested plantations of yew (*Taxus* spp., usually English yew *T. baccata*). This is a huge improvement on the early 1980s when tracts of Pacific yew (*T. brevifolia*) and Himalayan yew (*T. wallichiana*) were wiped out to collect the bark.

It is little known that the pharmaceutical industry has a much better conservation record than the herbal industry. Drugs are either planta-tion grown, rather than taken from the wild, or synthesized without using 'plant material'. Even if you count petrochemicals as long-dead plant material, the industry has the potential to continue manufacturing using plants sustainably by re-placing petrochemical sources for drug manufac-ture by 'pharmed' plants, that is plants genetically engineered to express therapeutic proteins.

It should be clear that plants are hugely important in drug *manufacture*, particularly in oncology. However, the pharmaceutical industry goes through cycles in its valuation of 'natural products' as sources for novel drug development. The American plant-screening programme of the 1950s and '60s resulted in the taxol and so-called vinca drugs (from *Catharanthus roseus*). Since then, totally synthetic 'combinatorial chemistry' has been the preferred research tool. The pendulum will at some stage return to the natural world as the source of chemical innovation. What is less clear is whether the research focus will change – from drugs for diseases of the developed world (cancer/heart disease/stroke) to the infectious diseases that are the killers in the developing world. Currently 90 per cent of research funds are spent in the developed world, which is home to only 10 per cent of the world's population.

Opium poppy seed heads

Lavender

Lavender belongs to the same botanical family (*Lamiaceae*) as mint, thyme, sage, basil and rosemary. Its name comes from the Latin *lavando*, part of the verb *lavare*, meaning to wash. Over two thousand years ago the Romans were adding this small purple-blue Mediterranean flower to their communal baths to ease their aching limbs. Since then lavender has served as a truly multipurpose herb, with uses ranging from lice repellent and corpse embalmer to highly prized French perfume, from pesticides to air fresheners, from antiseptic to sleep-inducer. Elizabeth I is known to have preferred lavender conserve with lamb above all else.

Lavender's essential oils vary enormously in composition, smell and quality. Climate, altitude and soil type all have a bearing on it. The oil is produced while the flower calyx (bud) is forming. As the sun warms the plant, the calyx perspires. The buds are harvested just before flowering, when the oil concentration is at its highest. The harvested lavender is left in the fields for a few days and then the essence is extracted using the ancient technique of distillation.

France has one of the largest areas of lavender under cultivation, but a wide variety of cultivars are now grown around the world by large-scale producers in Australia, Japan, New Zealand, the UK, the USA, Spain, Russia, Ukraine, Moldova, Bulgaria and China. In all there are about 36,500 hectares under cultivation, producing approximately 1,000 tonnes of lavendin oil, 150–200 tonnes of spike lavender oil and 200 tonnes of true lavender oil. On average, 100–130 kilograms of lavender flowers are needed to obtain 1 kilogram of essence.

True or English lavender (*Lavandula augustifolia*), with its wonderfully fine-scented oil which is used in perfumery and aromatherapy, is produced in large quantities in the UK, France, Australia, New Zealand and Japan. Lavandin (*L. x intermedia*, a hybrid of *L. augustifolia* and *L. latifolia*) can grow on poorer soils and produces far greater yields. It is mainly used for detergents and can be used in soap manufacture. It is not recommended for medical use. Introduced to Provence in the 1920s,

The Lavender exhibit at Eden

149

lavendin is the main type of lavender to be cultivated in France today. The international lavendin market is extremely competitive, the fluctuating essential oil prices resulting in low price margins for growers. Climate, soil and altitude are critical factors when considering the viability of large-scale planting. In addition, the quality and quantity of the oil need to remain consistent for several years in order to attract potential buyers.

The Greek physician Dioscorides (*c.* AD 40–90) was the first to note the medicinal properties of lavender. He recommended its use in a tea-like infusion for chest complaints and claimed it had laxative and invigorating qualities. Other classical physicians suggested using it as an antidote to poison and snake bites, and, taken with wine, in treating stomach ache, liver, renal and gall disorders, jaundice and dropsy. Pliny the Elder (*c.* AD 23–79) advocated lavender for bereavement as well as promoting menstruation. During the Middle Ages lavender became well established in the European medicine cabinet and was used for all manner of ailments. Its popularity only began to wane in the later part of the nineteenth century when modern medicine began to take a hold.

Today, interest in lavender as an alternative remedy is re-emerging and it is in widespread use in aromatherapy. Indeed, its use to relieve burns inspired the development of therapeutic aromatherapy in France. Although it is acknowledged that many of the older uses of lavender are more than simply old wives' tales, clinical trials have been investigating its efficacy with mixed results. However, it is known to exhibit central nervous system depressant activity; it may be helpful in gastro-intestinal disorders to reduce sugar and cholesterol levels; and it can help in skin-grafting surgery. Lately, lavender compound perillyl alcohol is being studied for its promising effects in cancer prevention.

I am burns' ease, I am wounds' nurse.
I am ages' scent, Heaven sent.
I am as purple as veins, I am a feeder of flames.
Annamaria Murphy

Plants for perfume

Sniff a fragrant rose, rub a piece of mint. How do these scents make us feel? Our sense of smell links to the oldest part of the brain, the limbic system, the centre for our emotions and memory. We can detect over ten thousand different odours.

Many of our perfumes and scents come from plant extracts. Plants, unable to embrace their partners or run away from danger, use scent to attract pollinators and repel predators. Pollinators, attracted by scented petals, often get a reward of nectar. Would-be predators are warned off by the wafts of aromatic gums and resins in some leaves.

So why do we use perfume? Like plants, is it to warn, signal or seduce, or is it for sweet memory and comfort? Smell is linked to our basic survival instincts, used to detect burning or rotten food for example, but it also arouses our central emotions, making us feel good and often stimulating a response in others. Twenty-five per cent of those who lose their sense of smell are said to lose their sex drive as well.

Smell is also connected to health. Aromatics were popular during the Black Death in the thirteenth century, as people thought the plague was transmitted by breathing foul air. Doctors wore pointed 'beak-shaped' nosegays, which were the origin of the term 'quack'. Today smell plays many roles in our well-being. Essential oils are used in aromatherapy through inhalation and application to the skin. Some of these have antibacterial and antiseptic properties. The smell of rosemary may raise alertness and that of spiced apples can reduce blood pressure in cases of stress.

One of the most extraordinary attributes of smell is that it triggers memory. Detecting perfume on a passer-by or in a flower bed can evoke strong memories. Some herbs go to the seat of emotions. Poets and writers say they gain inspiration from perfume. The writer Marcel Proust used to travel from Paris to Normandy, his childhood home, to smell the apple blossom. Children given a word list to learn recall the words more easily and retain them for longer when scents are used. The sense of smell is often the last sense to go in sufferers from Alzheimer's disease, and scent is sometimes used in its treatment.

Perfume originated in Mesopotamia, where it was used as incense (*per fumum*/by smoke) for the gods, as well as to sweeten rotten meat, in ceremonies, and medicinally. It also became part of the human emotional armoury. Egyptians placed perfumed waxed cones, which melted over their faces, under their wigs. Cleopatra, queen of perfume and power, wore '*kyphi*' (containing rose, crocus and violet) on her hands, and '*aegyptium*' (almond oil, honey, cinnamon,

Scent cones were worn by ancient Egyptians

Geranium oil

Geranium oil, from Morocco, France, Réunion Island and Italy, is one of the most important and valuable oils in perfumery. It has a leafy-earthy odour with rosy-minty overtones and a rich, long-lasting sweet-rosy base note. The oil is steam distilled from the leaves and stems of rose geranium (Pelargonium graveolens).

Jasmine oil

Jasminum grandiflorum 'De Grasse' is one of the most cultivated perfume ingredients in the world. To produce jasmine oil the flowers have to be handpicked at dawn before the light oils evaporate. It takes eight million jasmine flowers to produce 1 kilogram of oil.

Violet oil

Ionone, the rare and true violet oil from Viola 'Toulouse', short circuits our sense of smell. We momentarily lose our ability to smell it until the sense returns. Violet was Empress Josephine's favourite perfume. When she died, Napoleon planted violets on her grave and in exile on St Helena he kept some in a locket around his neck until the day he died.

orange and henna) on her feet. She also perfumed the purple sails of her barge. Greek writers recommended mint for the arms, thyme for the knees, cinnamon, rose and palm oil on the jaws and chest, almond oil on the feet and hands and marjoram on the hair and eyebrows.

Today around 20 per cent of the fragrance industry's income is derived from body perfumes, while 80 per cent comes from fragrances used in a wide variety of everyday products, from cars to shoe polish (subliminally arousing the desire to buy), as well as in food and drink manufacture.

Scents can be extracted from plants by expression (physical pressure), dry distillation (heat), steam distillation, gaseous or solvent extraction and the traditional method of enfleurage (in which flower petals are pressed into fat spread on to glass, then pressed in wooden racks). A new technique, called headspace, captures odours by placing glass bowls over fragrant plants. The odour pattern is then synthesized. This may not be 'natural' but it could be said to be environmentally friendly as it helps to prevent over-harvesting of wild species.

Making a perfume is like composing music. Grades of fragrance are often categorized using

a musical scale. The top note gives the first impression, the middle note the heart of the fragrance, and the base note the richer heavier scent, which gives it longevity. As in music composition, perfumers say that their creations come from dreams, travel, reading and inhaling the scents all around them. Monitoring responses to the finished product enables perfume-makers to understand its sensory characteristics. Scents can then be created and manufactured with a particular response in mind. Like music, the love of different scents is a question of personal taste and mood.

Equipment used for extracting plant scents

Tobacco

Tobacco and health have been on a strange journey together. Soon after landing on European shores the leafy herb was heralded as a cure-all before it took on the mantle of addictive drug and toxic carcinogen. Ironically, new research is once again looking to tobacco's curative potential.

Unlike its distant relations, the potato, tomato and sweet pepper, tobacco (*Nicotiana tabacum*) isn't tasty. How did people come to roll it up in bits of paper, set fire to it and inhale the smoke of the fifteen billion cigarettes we now light up every day? Native Americans, from the Mississippi to the Amazon, have been using the weed for centuries. Around 1500 BC the Mayans

Tobacco leaves drying in the sunshine

were smoking it as part of religious ceremonies and the pre-Columbian Native Americans took it before battle, hunting, peace talks and rituals. Christopher Columbus is credited with bringing tobacco to Europe in the late fifteenth century. Tobacco is still used as an important curing plant by Mesoamerican Indians today, usually taken as a snuff called San Pedro powder. In Mexico, shamans make tea from tobacco leaves for their patients, who then take part in a séance which culminates in a diagnosis by the shaman.

Tobacco relieves hunger, depresses the nervous system and is highly addictive. Some heroin addicts say it is harder to give up tobacco than heroin. Nicotine, found in tobacco, is thought to raise dopamine levels in the brain. This neurotransmitter is responsible for feelings of pleasure and persists for forty-five minutes or more. The next time the brain is stimulated the 'buzz' is greater. Increased exposure leads to an increase in sensitivity to the drug, not the reverse, as was previously thought. Nicotine affects the brain within ten seconds of inhalation. The immediate effects are increases in heart rate, blood pressure and hormone production, a constriction of the small blood vessels under the skin, and changes in blood composition and metabolism.

The reputed pleasures of tobacco were joined in the 1550s by accounts of its medicinal virtues. In Spain it was used to treat toothache, bad breath, worms, the plague and even cancer. By 1571 the list of ailments supposedly cured by tobacco had risen to nearly forty, but it wasn't long before the counterattack started. 'Smoking is a custom harmful to the brain, dangerous to the lungs, and in the black, stinking fume thereof nearest resembling the horrible Stygian smoke of the pit that is bottomless,' said James I of England. In 1665 Samuel Pepys commented on a cat dropping dead after being administered a drop of 'distilled oil of tobacco'. As early as 1868, a law was passed requiring railway companies to provide smoke-free carriages 'to prevent injury to non-smokers', and in 1904 a judge in New York sent a woman to jail for thirty days for smoking in front of her children. Others took the matter to further extremes: Sultan Murad IV executed smokers as infidels and Shah Sefi punished two tobacco merchants by pouring molten lead down their throats.

Cigarette smoke contains the poisons carbon monoxide, acetone, arsenic, ammonia, formaldehyde and hydrogen cyanide, as well as tar. Today we know that smoking kills three million people a year. By 2025, tobacco may kill as many people worldwide as dysentery, pneumonia, malaria and tuberculosis combined. Smoking is the greatest single cause of ill health and premature death in England. Until the 1930s lung cancer was a rare disease, but in 1950 the *British Medical Journal* reported that heavy smokers were fifty times as likely to die from lung cancer as non-smokers. Smoking is also related to cancers of the blood, nose, mouth, tongue, throat, bladder, stomach, kidneys and penis. It causes emphysema, increases the risk of heart attacks and can be a contributory factor in osteoporosis and defective vision. The Center for Disease Control in Atlanta estimated the health and productivity costs of smoking cigarettes in 2002 to be $3,391 per person per year, or $7.18 per pack.

'A cigarette is the perfect type of a perfect pleasure. It is exquisite, and it leaves one unsatisfied. What more can one want?'

Oscar Wilde

Tobacco also has adverse effects on the environment. The plant rapidly depletes the soil of nutrients and is prone to a wide variety of fungal, bacterial and viral diseases, so new, clean plots often have to be cleared for it each year. It is also frequently cured by burning wood, which causes further deforestation. In the Philippines thousands of hectares of tropical forest are cut down every year for tobacco.

To combat pests and diseases, each tobacco crop may be sprayed up to sixteen times with fungicides, insecticides and herbicides that are documented as causing health problems to farm workers as well as to the environment. These pesticides are persistent and have been found in cigarettes. Ironically, some tobacco companies are now marketing organic rolling tobacco.

Morals and money

James I was so concerned about the adverse effects of tobacco that he tried to destroy the tobacco trade by increasing import duty by 400 per cent, creating a bonanza for smugglers. Tax revenue needs then overcame his principles; he cut the duty by two-thirds and the trade rapidly increased. Louis XIV established a tobacco monopoly to maximize profits from the trade. African slaves were brought to America to plant tobacco and the first Thanksgiving day (13 December 1621) was held to celebrate a successful tobacco harvest. Benjamin Franklin used five million pounds of tobacco as collateral for a massive loan from France to help fund the American Revolution.

By 2002 the world was growing 5.7 million tonnes of tobacco, with the help of thirty-three million people from over one hundred countries, 80 per cent of which are in the developing world. Today the main tobacco-growing countries are China, the USA, Brazil, Turkey and Zimbabwe. Tobacco is potentially a profitable crop but, as with coffee, the small farmers are often the losers, more money being made further up the chain. Tobacco remains a major world commodity; an addictive drug that is a massive source of revenue gained from sales and advertising, export earnings and customs duty.

In 1998, the British government published a tobacco policy White Paper entitled *Smoking Kills*, designed to reduce tobacco use in Britain, which included proposals to tackle smoking in public places and the workplace. In Ireland and in many American states smoking has been banned in the workplace and all public spaces, including bars. In Britain health warnings now have to occupy at least 30 per cent of the front of a cigarette packet and 40 per cent of the back. In 2003 the British government brought tobacco advertising to an end. New tobacco sponsorship agreements, advertising on billboards, in the press, by free distributions, through direct mail or on the internet, and new promotions were banned.

The other side of the coin is that some scientific research identifies beneficial roles for nicotine. It is thought that smoking may help to alleviate some of the symptoms of disorders such as schizophrenia, Parkinson's disease and Alzheimer's.

There is a final irony to the tobacco story. Tobacco's ease of propagation, quick growth and high quantity of seed production make it the laboratory rat of the plant kingdom. Tobacco was one of the first plants to be genetically modified. Therapeutic proteins, used in the treatment of human disease, are generally produced in bacteria, cell culture or from human donors, but this can be very expensive and sometimes dangerous. Useful genes inserted into tobacco enable the plant to produce proteins and vaccines in the leaves for flavouring, fragrance or medicinal applications. Using tobacco in this way as a high-yield bio-factory may provide a viable alternative. It is yet another example of 'pharming', and could also give tobacco farmers a market other than the cigarette industry.

Tobacco is already being used to produce the enzyme glucocerebrosidase which is missing in people with Gaucher's disease, a rare genetic disorder causing brittle bones and even death. Scientists are developing a vaccine against tooth decay from GM tobacco and are also working on the production of a vaccine for non-Hodgkin's lymphoma, a cancer of the lymph system. The tobacco story has come full circle.

Tobacco harvest in Ecuador

157

Food and health

It is impossible to look at health without looking at food. We need to start with what we eat and the exercise we take before we even think about taking any curative measures.

In the UK we consume fewer calories today than we did in the 1940s, eating half the amount of fat and half the amount of bread but twice the amount of meat. However, as a nation and across the developing world we are getting bigger. This could be attributed to our sedentary lifestyle. Our use of cars, computer games and TV and long working hours means that we are less physically active. We are eating too many calories for our activity levels, which is leading in the West to the prospect of a generation of young people dying before their parents from the early onset of cardiovascular disease, diabetes, diet-related cancers and strokes through hypertension. In the West intake of food is becoming less and less linked with nutrition. It has always had a social/spiritual dimension (for example, the

Vietnamese pho *is a very healthy noodle soup*

'We are indeed much more than what we eat, but what we eat can nevertheless help us to be much more than what we are.'
Adelle Davis

Christian breaking of bread); now eating out is a major leisure/recreational activity. People have always eaten on the hoof but today's convenience food is high in fat and, particularly, high in salt, both of which have a negative effect on health. 'Comfort eating' is another major issue, linked with attempts to reduce excessive levels of stress. Nutrition is also linked to psychological eating disorders such as anorexia or bulimia. People eat when they are not hungry and don't stop when they are full, which is dysfunctional.

In the UK the government's White Paper on public health (2004) aims to tackle smoking, obesity, drinking and sexual and mental health. Recommendations include:

- By the end of 2008, all enclosed public places and workplaces to be smoke-free.
- By mid-2005, processed foods to be clearly labelled to indicate fat, sugar and salt content to shoppers.
- Children will be encouraged to cycle to school and adults to get active at work.
- The government to work to cut down binge drinking.

In underdeveloped countries malnutrition is probably produced not by total world shortages but by poor distribution, poverty and a range of other factors: trade rules at the beginning of the twenty-first century subsidize farmers in the West, leading to food dumping, undermining underdeveloped countries' agriculture; infra-structure and transport problems hinder food distribution in the developing world; natural cycles of drought plus climate change induce crop failure; AIDS and other diseases kill off farmers.

A healthy planet

Plants provide most of our resources: food, fuel, medicine, building materials and, in the last few years, genes. Plants and the broader ecosystems they belong to also supply something else: 'essential services'. These include:

- air conditioning
- climate control
- water purification and storage
- recycling
- maintenance of biodiversity

and also more abstract services, including:

- art and beauty
- provision for recreation and enjoyment
- learning and inspiration.

These contribute to the health of our global environment and ecosystems, the health of the plants we rely on and the health of each and every one of us.

The main ecosystems are:

- the green forests, both temperate and tropical
- the grasslands and deserts
- the ocean surfaces teeming with photo-synthesizing bacteria
- smelly oxygen-free sediments where bacteria rot things down
- the soils and soil life of the world
- our farms and managed forests.

Rainforests – a living carbon store

159

Biosphere Two in Arizona

One way of assessing the value of our natural ecosystems in terms of providing resources and services is to imagine moving to a barren environment such as the moon or Mars and working out what we would need to take with us to sustain our lives. A group of scientists attempted to do this in Arizona in the 1980s in Biosphere Two, a 1.2 hectare enclosed environment where eight people sealed themselves in and lived inside for two years. The project re-created several ecosystems inspired by our own that included forests and oceans as well as a farm and a garden. This valuable living experiment demonstrated the complexity of trying to re-create what to nature comes naturally. It showed, for example, the vital importance of recycling all waste to become a resource once again, of not using any toxic materials in construction that could release pollutants into their air and water, of thinking about every impact of every action and its effect on the whole system. We live on Biosphere One. Do we think in the same way?

Microscopic life, as well as plants, are a vital component of many of these ecosystems. This includes photosynthesizing bacteria (equivalent to tiny plants), consuming bacteria (equivalent to tiny animals) and the fermenters (which rot and recycle), all of which have been part of the essential services for the last 3,500 billion years.

It was not until we began to disrupt these services that we realized the knock-on effects and true costs of disrupting them. For example, deforestation can lead to flooding, a disrupted water cycle and disruption of our water purification and storage systems. Potential solutions may involve planting trees rather than constructing man-made flood defences, the equivalent of preventative rather than curative medicine. Another example is fossil fuels. Coal and oil increased productivity and wealth and brought freedom to many. They still do. But now the use of these has begun to show its dark side as the gases they produce are affecting climate change (see page 163).

Air conditioning

The air on our planet comes in four layers: the stratosphere, which lies below the thermosphere and mesosphere layers, creates the ozone layer, which protects us from ultra-violet radiation and breaks down methane, nitrous oxide and chlorofluorocarbons (CFCs). Ozone is made and destroyed by sunlight. CFCs enhance ozone's

Power station emissions are poisoning our atmosphere

destruction. Closer to home the troposphere contains 21 per cent oxygen, 79 per cent nitrogen, 0.03 per cent carbon dioxide, 1.7 p.p.m. methane, 1 per cent unreactive noble gases (argon, neon, xenon and krypton) and very small amounts of a few others. If there were no life on Earth, this cocktail of gases, along with the chemicals in the sea and on the land, would react together until no more change was possible, reaching a steady state. But because there is life the atmosphere is in a dynamic state. All life – that is, plants and animals (including us) – take oxygen out of the air to burn up (metabolize) food to produce energy. They return carbon dioxide to the air as a waste product. Carbon dioxide levels in the

'The human economy, as well as human health, depends upon the services performed "for free" by ecosystems. The ecosystem services supplied annually are worth many trillions of dollars. Economic development that destroys habitats and impairs services can create costs to humanity over the long term that may greatly exceed the short-term economic benefits of the development. These costs are generally hidden from traditional economic accounting, but are nonetheless real and are usually borne by society at large. Tragically, a short-term focus in land-use decisions often sets in motion potentially great costs to be borne by future generations. This suggests a need for policies that achieve a balance between sustaining ecosystem services and pursuing the worthy short-term goals of economic development.'

Dr Gretchen Daily, Stanford University, California

atmosphere are also increased when decomposing bacteria rot things down, when it's belched out of the molten belly of volcanoes and when fires burn. Fortunately for us, plants and some green bacteria act as living power stations by turning sunlight into the fuel (carbohydrate) that powers our bodies using carbon dioxide and water as raw materials. This process is called photosynthesis and the only waste product is oxygen. Together we all form a cycle that keeps the atmosphere in a suitable state.

Some believe that the tropical rainforest helps to increase oxygen levels in the air. Others think that this ecosystem uses all the oxygen it produces and that the photosynthesizing algae in the seas are the main oxygen producers. Although oxygen is vital for our survival, it is a tricky gas, speeding up the ageing process considerably. Some believe it to be carcinogenic and mutagenic (causing mutations) also. Animals and plants have evolved systems to

protect themselves from it, but oxygen limits how long we live. Small animals with high metabolic rates, such as mice, have shorter life spans than their larger cousins.

Human activity is changing the gases in the atmosphere. Since the Industrial Revolution burning fossil fuels has increased carbon dioxide levels by 33 per cent. Methane levels have more than doubled in the last two hundred years. Methane emissions come from landfill sites and livestock and rice farming as well as burning fossil fuels. The main challenge is not the direct effects of these emissions on air quality but their effects on the Earth's temperature.

Climate control

According to astrophysicists the sun has increased in luminosity by 25 per cent since life began, yet the Earth's temperature, despite a few fluctuations, has remained comfortable enough to sustain life for the last three and a half billion

Testing for greenhouse gases

years. In other words it's not as hot as it should be. Plants and their ecosystems may provide a buffering system, helping to regulate the Earth's temperature.

The planet's temperature is affected by its colour: dark places such as the northern forests absorb heat and get warmer; pale places such as deserts and tropical rainforests (which produce high white clouds) reflect heat and keep cooler. This phenomenon, known as the albedo effect, helps to regulate the planet's temperature. Economists have calculated that the Amazon's natural refrigeration unit is worth about $150 trillion.

The world's forests help to control the climate in many other ways too. They act as windbreaks, and insulators trapping warmth.

The greenhouse effect The atmosphere, with its 'greenhouse' gases (carbon dioxide, methane and water vapour), acts like a duvet, keeping the Earth's surface warm and protecting it from sunburn. The sun emits short light waves which pass through the atmosphere, hit the Earth and lose energy. The resulting longer infrared waves radiate back as heat. These wavelengths, having less energy that the short waves, are absorbed and re-radiated by the greenhouse gases. This is called the greenhouse effect, because it is exactly what happens in a greenhouse, the glass acting as a substitute for the Earth's 'greenhouse' gases. Without our greenhouse gases the Earth's temperature could be about −19°C. However, now that we are increasing the carbon dioxide and other greenhouse gases it may be getting hotter than we bargained for. We are already seeing hydro-metrological disasters driven by climate change – floods, storms, droughts, heatwaves, melting ice sheets, changing ocean currents and, in turn, landslides, rising sea levels, forest fires, atmospheric pollution, land degradation, changing cropping patterns, disruptions to ecosystems, biodiversity loss, water pollution, food security problems, displacement of people and other effects.

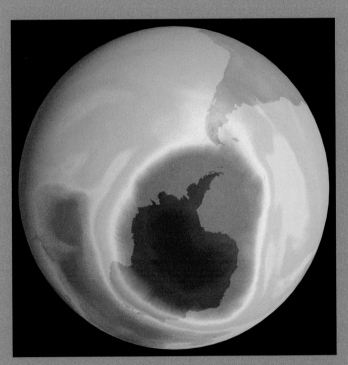

'While our planet's climate does vary naturally, the warming we have seen over the last 30 years seems to be due to increasing concentrations of carbon dioxide and other greenhouse gases in the atmosphere caused by our burning of fossil fuels and deforestation. If our greenhouse gas emissions continue unchecked, we expect this warming to continue in the future, leading to other effects such as changes in rainfall patterns. The local climates we are used to may change into less familiar states – the past is no longer a guide to the future. The changes in CO_2 levels over the last 150 years are not a blip. CO_2 is now higher than it has been over at least the last 440,000 years.'
Meteorological Office, 2004

Carbon storage What do chalky cliffs and rainforests have in common? They both help to cool the planet by locking up carbon dioxide (CO_2). Rainforests extract CO_2 from the air and fix the carbon in their woody bodies. The ocean algal ecosystems also act as huge CO_2 sinks. Some of the algae, called diatoms and coccolithospores, have tiny shells that are made of calcium carbonate (which contains a lot of carbon). When they die these sink to the ocean floor, to appear as limestone cliffs when the Earth heaves them up. Rock weathering also gets rid of CO_2. CO_2 dissolved in water reacts with calcium silicate from volcanic rock to give calcium bicarbonate and silicic acid. These compounds end up as calcium carbonate and silica on the ocean floor and eventually turn into limestone (calcium carbonate) rock strata.

Reducing emissions The Kyoto Protocol (which was adopted in 1997 and which came into force in 2005) includes commitments by thirty-eight developed countries to reduce their annual emissions of greenhouse gases (by an average of 5.2 per cent below emissions recorded in the baseline year of 1990) between 2008 and 2012. This is a step in the right direction but it is widely accepted that reductions need to be much greater to have any effect on climate change (for example, an 8 million tonne reduction in greenhouse gases, rather than 1 million).

Ideas for reducing carbon emissions include energy efficiency and energy conservation by using more efficient vehicles, making fewer journeys, building efficient buildings, building efficient coal plants and looking to alternative fuel sources. Many available plant fuels are potentially carbon neutral: when they regrow they take in the same amount of carbon dioxide as the amount they release when they burn. These fuels include wood, used for fuel worldwide; crops grown specifically for fuel; coppiced willow, miscanthus and bamboo; agricultural wastes such as straw and sugar cane waste, and biofuels – bioethanol from sugar cane, biodiesel from rape seed, biomethanol from wood residues (see page 219).

Carbon trading Carbon trading is a tool to help limit and eventually reduce emissions. The concept is based on the fact that a tonne of carbon dioxide (or other polluting gas) causes the same damage wherever it is released. First, governments decide between themselves how much each country should be allowed to emit. Then they issue licences to businesses and factories, allowing them to emit a set level of carbon dioxide (or other pollutant).

If a business becomes more efficient, it can sell its licences to others. This creates an incentive to reduce emissions. A business that is going to go over its limit (for example because it has an extra large order) can buy licences from others with some to spare, or from projects that work to reduce emissions, such as energy efficiency projects, renewable fuel projects or forestry. This funds and encourages the uptake of less polluting technology. The total number of licences to emit is reduced over time.

So far, only some countries have signed up to do this under the Kyoto Protocol (the USA and Australia being notable exceptions). A Europe-wide trading scheme started on 1 January 2005.

Mega-engineering Some climate scientists feel that governments are not doing enough to solve the problem of increasing carbon dioxide levels, and have been looking at major, global-scale solutions, known as mega-engineering, in which technology is developed to combat problems brought about by technology. Recent ideas have come from two main concepts: either to capture carbon dioxide and store it out of harm's way, or to allow it to accumulate but deflect the heat from the sun back into space. Suggestions of ways to achieve the latter include placing in the sea giant whisks that throw salt spray into the atmosphere to whiten clouds, spraying sulphate into the atmosphere to create clouds and using giant mirrors and aluminium balloons to reflect the light.

Water purification

We need to consume at least 2 litres of water a day for our bodies to function properly. Seventy per cent of our planet is covered by water. Of this, 97 per cent is too salty to drink. Of the remaining 3 per cent much is locked in ice and snow. Overall, of the estimated 1.3–1.4 billion cubic kilometres of water that exist in the world, less than 1 per cent is fresh water that is available for our use: that's one teaspoon out of a bucketful.

Most of our available fresh water comes in the form of rain. About 119,000 cubic kilometres of rain falls on the Earth every year – enough to cover the land a metre deep all over – but it is not evenly distributed.

The sun evaporates water from the salty seas to make clouds, creating pure, clean water vapour. On (wet) land plants give a helping hand to this rainmaking process by taking water up from the soil, passing it through their bodies and out through their leaves (that is, by transpiration). The sun evaporates water from small holes in the plant's leaves (stomata), which open when the sun comes out, and this action sucks water up the plant's trunk through tiny tubes. In the Amazon, 50 per cent of the rainfall is recycled in the forest itself in this way. Deforestation could reduce the rainfall in this part of the world to such an extent that the Earth's climate may never recover. Marine algae (the coccoliths) are also rainmakers. They produce sulphur gases (dimethyl sulphide) which act as nuclei to start cloud formations.

Fresh water is stored underground in soils, plant roots and aquifers (natural underground reservoirs) and above ground in rivers, lakes and reservoirs. Disruption to this storage system by, for example, careless planning, pollution through agriculture or removal of plant cover, such as deforestation, can be very damaging.

Rain clouds over the Amazon

165

Water issues Sulis, Sisiutl, Chalchiuhtlicue and Analinda are just some of the names given to the spiritual embodiment of water in cultures as diverse as Celtic, Native American, Aztec and Persian. Yet although water is central to life and recognized as a basic human right, today more than 1 billion people do not have access to clean water and 2.6 billion do not have adequate sanitation. Unlike running out of oil or gas, if we run out of water there are no alternatives.

Asia is home to 60 per cent of us yet has only 36 per cent of global water resources, while Latin America, with 6 per cent of the world's population, has access to over 25 per cent of global water resources. Approximately 480 million people are already living in water-stressed regions and conservative estimates suggest that by the middle of this century this figure will increase to 2 billion in nearly fifty countries.

Water-related diseases are the single largest cause of human sickness and death in the world, and they disproportionately affect the poor. A child dies every fifteen seconds as a result of poor access to clean water; that's equivalent to the number of deaths caused by 6,000 full jumbo jets crashing every year. Ninety per cent of deaths from diarrhoeal diseases are children under the age of five. Fifty per cent of global hospital beds are occupied by people suffering from water-borne diseases such as cholera, typhoid, polio, hepatitis A and B, meningitis, dysentery and other diarrhoeal diseases.

More than five million people die every year from preventable water-related diseases. Women and children, the main water carriers in countries where it needs to be fetched, are at greatest risk. The diseases associated with poor water and sanitation – tuberculosis, bilharzia, yellow fever, sleeping sickness and dengue fever – are varied and widespread. Many can be prevented by the provision of clean water, sanitation and good hygiene practices.

The economic cost of water-related diseases, particularly in developing countries, can also be

Searching for water in Mali

crippling. In sub-Saharan Africa alone, malaria costs $1.7 billion a year in medical treatment and lost productivity. Peru lost approximately $232 million in just one year following a cholera outbreak. Economic growth in developing countries is slowed by about 1.3 per cent as a result of poor health.

In the last hundred years the global population has tripled but demand for water has increased sevenfold. Agriculture uses 70 per cent of all withdrawn fresh water, and the irrigated area increases year by year, much of it ruining the land by increased salinization (caused by water evaporating and leaving the salts behind in the soil). Eighty per cent of Mexico City's water is withdrawn from one aquifer. As a result the land is shifting and Mexico City is sinking. We use more water irrigating golf courses around the globe than it would take to provide half the world's population with the UN-recommended amount of water. In the West we pressurize water companies continually to improve the quality of our drinking water, and then flush that same water down our toilets.

Urban populations are growing. By 2020 60 per cent of us will live in cities. As the demand for water in urban areas increases so too will the pressure to divert resources from rural areas. A recent study looked at the additional water required to alleviate hunger and malnutrition by 2025 and found that the amount is equivalent to all water withdrawn at present for human society's use.

Water futures More people are gaining access to clean water and sanitation than ever before, although the rate at which they are doing so is not yet keeping up with the rate of population increase. Water issues have climbed up the political agenda, however, and an increasing number of organizations and governments are trying to address the problems.

Water is used to produce agricultural and industrial products. This 'virtual water' is moved around the globe every time a product is imported or exported. By being aware of the amount of water needed to produce each item, water-scarce countries can save their precious supplies by importing items with a high water input rather than trying to produce them domestically. This trade in virtual water is inherent in the global movement of goods, but there are suggestions that it should be formalized and taken into account in any water, food or environment policies, particularly in water-scarce countries.

Crop irrigation – draining the world's water supplies?

Around 50 per cent of water can be wasted through evaporation or run-off from traditional irrigation. Drip irrigation, where water is delivered directly to plant roots, can improve efficiency by 30–70 per cent. Currently 1 per cent of irrigated land uses this system. We can also make better use of our waste water. In Israel 70 per cent of sewage discharge is used, after preliminary treatment, for irrigation. Coastal cities in developing countries often discharge waste water directly into the ocean; 18,000 litres per second are discharged from the Peruvian capital, Lima, into the Pacific.

Desalinization is expensive and uses a lot of energy. New innovative technologies that deal with this problem include a plastic membrane that lets water vapour through but not dissolved salts, and the 'sea water greenhouse' that turns sea water into fresh water using the sun.

Another solution is to grow crops that are drought-resistant and can cope with saline soils. The ICRISAT (International Crops Research Institute for the Semi-Arid Tropics) Desert Margins programme is a case in point. ICRISAT is one of the international Future Harvest centres, with a headquarters in India and stations in the dry regions of Africa. It works on the semi-arid tropics (regions with over a billion people who each year have to survive in conditions of high temperatures and short, unreliable rainy seasons) on a range of crops including pearl millet (the most drought-resistant cereal grown on large areas of Africa and the desert regions of the Indian subcontinent), sorghum (which withstands drought and flooded soils), finger millet (a short-season cereal that can succeed after one significant rainfall), groundnuts and chickpeas bred to continue to grow into the dry season of semi-arid tropics and a range of short, quick-maturing varieties of legumes.

All of these crops have been bred at ICRISAT to cope with a range of conditions in areas that would previously have been considered unsuitable for crops, and into the dry season when the land was previously left fallow, or to be pest- and disease-resistant so avoiding the need for pesticides. ICRISAT is also pioneering the management of the land layout – 'Water Harvesting' – to catch any rainfall that does occur and allow it to soak into the subsoil. They have even bred a drought-resistant variety of rice. Drought-resistant cereals are generally able to cope with the higher salt levels (found on the otherwise fertile black soils in vast areas of the semi-arid tropics such as in Sudan), although legumes are less well adapted.

Social solutions are often intricately linked to the environmental ones, an example being the importance of collaboration over the use of shared water resources. During times of conflict or political disagreement, those working on water issues are often the only ones who continue a dialogue across the divide. The Arab Water Council was formed in 2004 in an endeavour 'to promote better understanding and management of the water resources in the Arab States … sharing experience and information … for the benefits of its inhabitants'.

Rainforests make rain, and rain makes rainforests

169

Soil – a vital resource

Recycling

Nature operates an efficient recycling service. We have seen that plants recycle carbon by taking in carbon dioxide for photosynthesis, and clean and recycle water by making pure water vapour (clouds) and therefore rain.

The soil is part of the recycling service. Soil is more than ground-up rocks. It is a food store, a reservoir of water and air, a foundation for the plant world and a home for the unsung heroes; the soil under a square metre of grassland contains about fifty thousand worms, fifty thousand mites and insects, twelve million roundworms and billions and billions of

bacteria. This hidden volunteer army is the nutrient recycling force. When plants and animals die, bacteria, fungi and other decomposers turn them into humus and simple inorganic chemicals; in other words, they rot them down. The fertilizer they make has all the right nutrients, in all the right proportions, because the raw material of that fertilizer is dead plants. Tiny particles of humus and clay in the soil carry electrical charges that hold on to nutrients, preventing them from being washed out of the soil by rain, so they can be taken up by the plants. Humus also acts as the glue that holds the soil together.

Soil fertility has caused civilizations to flourish or fail. Agro-ecosystems cover more than one quarter of the global land area, but almost 75 per cent of the land has poor soil fertility and about 50 per cent has steep terrain, constraining production. We push this land harder than nature, taking one or more crops off it a year. The fertility has to be returned. To speed things up many farmers use soluble artificial fertilizers, made using fossil fuels, which are taken up by the plant direct, bypassing the soil life. Advantages often include higher yields and lower amounts of labour requirements than systems that apply bulk organic fertilizers. Disadvantages include using up non-renewable resources, lack of organic matter in the soil (and therefore humus) leading to erosion and the leaching (washing out) of fertilizers, which causes pollution. The plants are also often more susceptible to pests and diseases (artificial fertilizers not always providing the balanced diet which is needed for good health). Nitrogen is one of the main soil nutrients that plants need, but it is in short supply on both the land and sea. Farmers spend millions on artificial nitrogen fertilizers to enhance plant growth, which is ironic in view of the fact that almost 80 per cent of our atmosphere is comprised of this gas, although most plants are unable to use it in this form. Employing a linear system that uses non-renewable resources and produces waste breaks nature's cycles.

'Waste is the unused output of a system.'

Soil Association

Solutions to these challenges include imitating nature's cycle, by applying compost to the soil to increase humus as well as nutrient levels and by planting crops such as legumes which make their own nitrogen fertilizer (see page 89). Fifty years after the Green Revolution (see page 80) some are calling for a science-led revolution to take agriculture forward using more advanced artificial fertilizers and pesticides. Others favour a modernized system

but with the cyclic approach. Others believe we can integrate both systems. Can the cyclic approach feed our ever-increasing population? For how long can the linear approach feed the world? The debate will continue.

Green glue Plant roots join humus in providing a very sticky service: holding the soil together across the planet. In nature bare soil is soon covered with vegetation: first with 'weeds', then with pioneer species, then a whole medley that arrive and take root.

Remove this green glue and wind and water can blow and wash the soil away. Around 15.9 million hectares of land (18 per cent of the total) are affected by soil erosion. Out of these, 11,172,000 hectares are affected by water erosion, while 4,760,000 hectares are affected by wind erosion. Loss of soil is one problem and where it goes is another. It can impair drainage, dirty water supplies, and block navigation systems and hydroelectric reservoirs. Silted-up reservoirs cost around $6 billion a year to fix. Removing the green glue also leads to leaching of nutrients, which can lead to contamination of water sources.

A simple solution is to replant denuded areas with trees and herbaceous plants to stabilize the soil. The first forest reserve in the western hemisphere was set up on the island of Tobago by legislators concerned about water conservation – in the 1780s. In many agricultural systems green manures are used: these are plants that are grown to hold the soil together and fertilize it when they are dug in prior to planting a crop. Adding organic matter (rotting plant and animal waste) to the soil is also important, as when it forms humus it will help to bind the particles.

No-tillage (no-dig) systems and contour planting (planting trees along contours between rows of crops on soil prone to erosion) can also help. At Eden the West Africa section in the Humid Tropics Biome shows a contour planting system using leguminous trees and vetiver grass (*Vetiveria zizanioides*) to hold the slopes together. In Eden's Outdoor Biome, which is planted on the steep slopes of the china clay pit, a combination of coir matting and a 'soup' of plant seed and plant nutrient sprayed on to the slopes knitted them together to hold the newly manufactured soil in place. People are turning more and more to such eco-engineering solutions to assist civil engineering techniques.

Waste Neutral Many useful materials that you use every day don't need to be discarded after just one use. They can enter a cycle and be used over and over again. Aluminium dug from the ground in tropical rainforests and plastics made from fossil fuels are good examples of this. The resources are non-renewable and the materials don't rot – contributing to our waste problem. Humans have therefore created a new cycle to deal with stuff like this.

The concept developed at Eden is called Waste Neutral. First and foremost, we reduce the amount of waste we produce. We then re-use where possible, before recycling the remainder.

Finally, we make recycled materials our purchasing priority for use on site or for sale in the shop. We reinvest.

When we buy an equal or greater weight of products made from recycled materials than the weight of materials sent to be recycled and for disposal, we will have reached Waste Neutral. This concept can be applied to any organization, community or even individual household. It operates as a cycle within the greater global system. It helps to reduce the amount of new materials used and also works with paper, glass and other metals, saving energy by recycling them rather than starting production from scratch.

Maintaining biodiversity

Biodiversity is essential to our well-being (see page 30). For example, many animals perform a vital service for a healthy planet: controlling pests. Pests destroy between a quarter and one-half of the world's crops. Chemical controls have many benefits but pests can become resistant to

Trees stabilize our soils

them. In nature, over 90 per cent of pests are controlled by natural predators, including birds, parasitic wasps and spiders.

Pesticide use has increased by over 200 per cent in the last twenty years. Of course modern pesticides are rigorously tested and much safer than earlier ones, and we have a much better understanding of the need for ecological balance, but it is almost impossible to 'prove' that adverse effects could not arise from a novel chemical.

Many developed countries have brought in regulations to stem the tide of chemicals entering the food chain through pesticide use, but developing countries are still being sold strong solutions with little guidance or protection. Ironically, the chemicals are often 'reimported' as residue on food crops. Environmental organizations are calling on the large agri-chemical conglomerates to halt production of such harmful pollutants and to develop a more responsible approach to their business. Meanwhile environ-

mental methods of pest control are being tried, including making the best of natural predators; using field margins to encourage biodiversity without affecting the yield; and planting a range of crop varieties rather than monocropping. One of the many important roles of biodiversity is therefore in pest control.

The abstract services

'Look deep into nature, and then you will understand everything better.'

Albert Einstein

Simply making contact with plants and the natural world is good for the health. A growing number of health practitioners are working with environmental organizations in order to offer nature-based activities as part of their healthcare programmes.

The obvious value of connection is that it encourages physical activity. Sedentary lifestyles are typical in urban populations, and there is increasing interest in the question of what motivates people to undertake exercise, even if it is only walking, for instance. Research points to the value of plants as incentives to elderly people to walk trails. Gardening is also a major stimulus for exercise amongst the middle-aged and elderly population.

Young people's contact and play in the natural environment has been shown to be valuable in developing skills. Through playing with natural environments children start to understand life cycles, birth and death, seasonality, cause and effect, begin to recognize patterns and systems, and experiment with the properties of materials. They learn to appreciate the importance of the health of their environment.

For many people active involvement with plants and gardening involves the motivation to care for and be responsible for a living object and requires the use of a range of different skills. This combination of motivation together with

Natural predators can help control pests

the scope for practising varying levels of mental and physical tasks provides the basis for the discipline known as horticultural therapy. That recovery from mental health problems can be accelerated by active outdoor work has been recognized for nearly two hundred years. As well as teaching skills, such as volume judgement when watering, and feeling the reward associated with success, gardening teaches people to interact positively with their environment and to effect changes. It therefore empowers them and helps build self-esteem.

Passive contact with nature, such as gazing at views, also influences health and well-being. Some research studies in this field have had wide and far-reaching implications: prison inmates are healthier with views of nature, and hospital patient recovery is speeded up by views of a tree rather than a treeless urban scene. One hypothesis about the causes of these passive health benefits relates to the effect of vegetation and natural scenes on stress levels. Stress is linked to many health problems and is found to reduce when certain natural settings are visited or just viewed. This field of research is evolving in parallel with an increasing interest among medics in the issue of how to maintain health rather than just treat sickness. The level of conviction has developed to such a point that more hospitals are being built with gardens to take account of the research.

It's all common sense, really: plants and landscapes can offer simple but effective opportunities for improving physical and mental well-being. Both gardens and wild places can give us pleasure and bring psychological healing through our five senses, either physically or indirectly via memories and mood. It is significant that the original meaning of the Persian word *paradisio*, from which the word paradise derives, is 'walled garden'.

'Climb up on some hill at sunrise.
Everybody needs perspective once
in a while, and you'll find it there.'
Robb Sagendorph

175

Voices on a healthy planet

In 2005 the Millennium Ecosystem Assessment report (MA) was released. This report, drawn up by 1,300 researchers from 95 nations over four years at the cost of some US $20 million, is a comprehensive survey of the state of the planet; a global inventory of our natural resources. It is intended to inform global policy initiatives and concludes that human activities threaten the Earth's ability to sustain future generations.

'When we look at the drivers of change affecting ecosystems, we see that, across the board, the drivers are either staying steady or increasing in severity – habitat change, climate change, invasive species, overexploitation of resources, and pollution.'
                                                                            Dr William Reid, director of the MA

'This report is an audit of nature's economy, and shows we've driven most of the accounts into the red ...
If you do this, ultimately there are significant consequences for our capacity to achieve our dreams in terms of poverty reduction and prosperity.'
                                                                    Jonathan Lash, World Resources Institute

The report puts forward a range of models designed to ease the strains on nature and evaluates how effective they may be. They include changing the way we consume, improving education and new technologies, paying for any ecosystem exploitation, and making ecosystem health a policy goal. Many of these policies require politicians to think long term and to develop economic indicators for environmental health.

'The range of current responses are not commensurate with the nature, the extent or the urgency of the situation that is at hand ... In our scenarios, we see that with interventions that are strategic, targeted, and more fundamental in nature we can realize some of the desired outcomes and they can have positive results for ecosystems, their services and human well-being.'
                                                            Angela Cropper, co-chair of the MA assessment panel

James Lovelock in his book *Gaia, The Practical Science of Planetary Medicine* describes the Earth as a single physiological system (including life and its environments, oceans, atmosphere and rocks) which, like living organisms, self regulates its chemistry and temperature in a state favourable for its inhabitants (see page 159). For years, he has been saying that we are pushing this system to its limits. To regulate, the planet may need to give us a kick!

Some say that we can use technology (e.g. giant whisks to create clouds and enormous sky mirrors to reflect the sun's rays) to address the problems that have been caused by technology. Lovelock rejects the idea of humans dominating and managing the Earth and proposes instead, 'that we live with the Earth as part of it; by managing ourselves, and by humbly taking and giving the gifts that sustain all of us who live on this planet'. He says, 'we are not masters of the Earth, we are the shop stewards, workers chosen, because of our intelligence, as representatives for the others ... the rest of life on our planet.'

Health – food for thought

*'Nature is man's teacher. She unfolds her treasures to his search, unseals his eye,
illumes his mind, and purifies his heart; and influence breathes
from all the sights and sounds of her existence.'*

Alfred Billings Street (1811–1881)

The World Heath Organization defines health as 'a state of complete physical, mental and social well-being and not merely the absence of disease or infirmity'. This is a provocative concept that instantly forces an awareness of the gulf between what we provide, or conceive of, as 'health services' and what we actually need. That this definition is promoted by an organization that works daily to tackle the almost unimaginable challenges presented by disease and malnutrition is even more sobering.

What is certainly clear is that the natural world does much more than supply us with medicines and other materials that provide cures. It even does more than provide our food for healthy bodies, and the services that maintain a healthy environment. Somehow to move towards this concept of health, on a societal as well as a personal level, requires us to re-examine the fundamentals of our relationship with the natural world, and to learn from the models that nature presents as well as the products.

Materials

The materials that make up the fabric of our lives are either grown or mined. This is no less true today than it was thousands of years ago, but there is a trend for increasing complexity in materials, with the result that it is harder and harder to recognize the origins of much of what we use. The innovations in technology that surround us, especially those that come from the digital age, rely in most cases on breakthroughs in the combinations of raw materials, whether through polymerization (making plastics) or the making of other forms of composites.

Superficially the environmental movement has tended to focus on the renewability of resources rather than on the critical issues of efficiency, waste and pollution and the impacts of extraction. Timber can be produced in an energy-efficient way, sustaining the quality of land and biodiversity, or it can be dragged indiscriminately from forests without concern for the protection of the tree species itself and the wildlife that depends on them, or for the conservation of the soil beneath. Natural fibres can be produced using benign production systems or with the use of huge amounts of energy, pesticides and artificial fertilizers.

Similarly, using quarried stone for a cottage that stands for centuries is a benign use compared with using materials extracted from a heavily polluting mine to make a complex hi-tech gadget that becomes rapidly obsolescent and proves almost impossible to recycle. Modern materials and modern design frequently offer the potential for huge efficiency gains (the Eden Biomes, for example, enclose enormous volumes with a relatively small amount of steel).

Energy is an even more complex matter. Advances in physics have opened up entirely new sources of energy, such as nuclear energy and photovoltaics, but still the vast majority of the world's fuels trace back to plants or Earth resources.

The dominant issue of energy use in the twenty-first century is to do not with the costs (economic, social and environmental) and impacts of extraction, high as they may be, but rather with the costs of use. The utilization of fossil fuels has a by-product of carbon dioxide production that, through climate change, threatens to be the most devastating pollutant of all (see page 163).

This threat has led to renewed interest in short-cycle natural fuels such as biodiesel made from plants. There are many problems to be solved before they can be viable cost-effective alternatives to fossil energy, but the driver to develop them is that the carbon dioxide they release through use is, theoretically, counter-balanced by the carbon dioxide they trap from the air while the plants from which they are made are growing.

This chapter looks at the current state of play with plant-derived materials and energy, both of

Traditional stone building

which have been vital in the past and are likely to play a vital role in our future. Technology could be described as the art and science of using materials in clever ways that open up new worlds of possibility and allow us to do things that were never within reach before. Technology drives the consumption of materials, providing us with goods and services that are so desirable that everyone must have them. One of the greatest challenges of the twenty-first century will be to service the demand for technology that comes from developing economies without magnifying the problems that we already see from uncontrolled consumption. One of the keys to meeting this challenge will be to make technology ever more efficient, and it is gradually becoming understood that the best models for doing so exist in nature. We finish this chapter therefore with a look at biomimicry – learning from how living organisms function rather than simply using them as providers of raw materials.

Over time, particularly in the West, the traditional use of plant-based materials has largely been overtaken by the use of cheaper and often more efficiently quarried, mined or manufactured materials. Today there are signs of change. Traditional materials are back in fashion and fossil-fuel-derived products are frowned upon. The construction industry is taking steps to reduce the volume of waste it is notorious for producing, turning to sustainable construction materials that are made more efficiently from renewable resources. Research is also looking to new bio-composite materials.

Dwellings in Namibia

Forest certification

Sustainable forestry is a method of managing forests to ensure that the 1.6 billion cubic metres of wood harvested each year can continue to meet demand. Forest certification identifies the key elements of sustainable forest management and creates criteria by which forest owners can certify their forests. This system introduces a minimum standard for forest management, independently assessed and verified, and enables timber products from certified forests to be marketed as such, raising standards in the process. In northern Europe many timber companies are now producing certified wood. In the tropics fewer incentives and illegal logging means the response to the system is much lower.

There are several certification schemes, of which the best-known in the UK is the Forest Stewardship Council (FSC), an independent, non-profit-making, non-governmental organization, an association of members from environmental groups, the timber trade and the forestry profession and other interested parties who promote responsible forestry through FSC certification and labelling. The FSC certification scheme makes it possible for buyers to choose products that come from forests managed to the highest environmental and social standards and from legal sources. It is the only scheme supported by the World Wildlife Fund and Greenpeace.

The temperate regions

Timber

At the beginning of the twenty-first century over 70 per cent of the people in the developed world still live in houses with timber frames. These are mainly found in North America, Scandinavia, Japan and Australia. Timber-framed houses perform well both environmentally and operationally. Timber is light, doesn't need wet mixing, uses less energy than concrete and plaster. It takes carbon dioxide in during its construction rather than releasing it as cement and concrete do. One problem with timber is that some woods need treating against fungal attack, but natural sugars can be removed from the wood, thus reducing this problem. Most of the timber used in general construction today comes from plantations in Russia, northern Europe and North America and mainly comprises softwood species such as pine, spruce, larch and Douglas fir. Panelling products such as plywood, strawboard, chipboard, fibreboard and veneer are made from both northern European and North American softwoods and tropical hardwoods.

Glue-laminated timber, or glulam, is favoured in construction for its structural strength, its enormous adaptability to different applications and its more sustainable impact on the environment. Glulam is formed by the bonding together of selected, planed layers of timber of parallel-running grain. The controlled selection of laminates means that weaknesses such as knots can be removed. Higher-quality material can be placed on the outer edges of the structure where the curve will be at its greatest and weaker, lower-quality material can be put in the inner layers, thus reducing wastage.

One of the strongest structural materials per unit of weight, glulam provides an excellent alternative to steel or concrete superstructures as

Timber-framed houses in Sweden

Eden's new Education Centre features a glulam roof structure made from red spruce (Picea rubens)

its lightness requires less foundation work and can be made to whatever shape or size is required. It can be used over spans of more than 50 metres, straight or curved (or, in the case of Eden's new Education Centre, double curved), which makes it suitable for every type of building.

The frame of the roof of Eden's Education Centre is made from red spruce (*Picea rubens*). The trees are sustainably grown and harvested from certified forests in Switzerland, where the roof was made. The forests are within 100 kilometres of the production plant. For the entire roof structure 400 cubic metres of glulam beams were needed, which required 1,000 cubic metres of timber – an estimated one hour's growth of the entire forested area of Switzerland. Red spruce reach between 20 and 25 metres tall and are harvested after 80–120 years' growth.

What wood for what?

Ash (*Fraxinus excelsior*), strong and flexible, has greater impact strength than any other home-grown hardwood. Used for anything from spears and shields in Anglo-Saxon times to the wings of the Second World War de Havilland Mosquito aircraft, it is still used for tool handles, furniture, new frames for Morgan sports cars and replacement frames for Morris Minors, sports equipment, walking sticks, tent pegs, the best traditional shepherd's crook, oars, gates and wheel rims.

Alder (*Alnus glutinosa*) is light, soft and water-resistant. Its main uses were in water pipes and piles under bridges, watercourse structures and sluice gates. Much of Venice was built on alder piles, and in Holland it was thought to be the

Willow for basketwork

Oak trees supplied 'the wooden walls of England'

best wood for clogs, being a poor conductor of heat. Nowadays it is mostly used for making charcoal and electric guitar bodies.

Willow (*Salix* spp.) was used for coracles and fast sailing boats, artificial limbs and toys. Today it is still employed for basketwork and, of course, the cricket bat made from the cricket bat willow (*Salix alba* subsp. *caerulea*).

English Oak (*Quercus robur*) is the main hardwood timber tree in Europe, used in construction for 9,000 years in Germany and 7,200 years in Ireland. John Evelyn said, 'To enumerate now the incomparable uses of this wood … the land and the sea do sufficiently speak of this excellent material; houses and ships, cities and navies are built with it.' Despite all this the main use was for tanning; around 90,000 tonnes of oak bark were used a year, equivalent to approximately 500,000 tonnes of felled trees – twice the amount used for ship building. Today oak is used in interior joinery – doors, windows, panelling and furniture – and still, being impervious and flexible, in boat building.

Holly (*Ilex aquifolium*), which is so dense it sinks in water, is used in inlay work, such as decorated furniture, chess pieces, hammers in harpsichords and butts of billiard cues.

English Yew (*Taxus baccata*), heavy and elastic, was used for longbows and spears. One of the world's oldest wooden artefacts is a 150,000-year-old spear found in Clacton, Essex. Yew fence posts are said to outlive iron, and the Vikings used yew nails for their ships. Today yew is more commonly employed in parquet floors, turned objects, furniture and veneers.

Beech (*Fagus sylvatica*) gives its name to the word 'book': beech blocks were once used to write on. Good for smoking herrings and to

make charcoal for gunpowder, beech also made the piles under Waterloo Bridge and Winchester Cathedral. Today it is used for turning, tool handles, furniture, sports equipment, kitchen utensils and chopping boards.

Black poplar (*Populus nigra*) was once used to line carts and make shields, being light, tough, splinter-resistant and shock-absorbing. Nowadays it is used for pallets, packing cases and matches.

Scots pine (*Pinus sylvestris*) is one of the strongest softwoods, used for joinery and construction. When treated it is used for telegraph poles, fencing, pit props and gateposts. In the Russian Arctic it was used to make roads.

Elm (*Ulmus* spp.) is long-lasting in water and was used for water pipes and bridge piles; and in boat building, for rudders and keels, the bottoms of canal barges, trawler boards and bobbins. It is used for furniture, decorative turnery, coffins and cart-wheel hubs.

Silver birch (*Betula pendula*), dismissed in the seventeenth century by John Evelyn as 'of all other the worst of timber', was said to be fit only for plywood, upholstery, framing and domestic items, and traditionally used for bobbins, spools and reels for the Lancashire cotton industry. It is still used today for traditional broomsticks, for stirring molten copper in copper refineries (to prevent formation of copper oxides), for parquet tiles and for panelling, and its brushwood is used on racecourse fences.

Non-timber construction materials

Traditionally reeds, wheat and straw were used for thatching roofs. Today the construction industry is seeing a renewed interest in plant-based building materials, including some new ones.

Timber is used in domestic joinery

Some examples of non-timber construction materials

The use of such materials has several important benefits: it reduces the impact of construction on the environment; it adds value to existing crops by using waste materials or developing new crops; and many of the materials have environmental benefits such as allergen reduction. Research is looking at finding the most suitable plants for insulation, paints, floor coverings, thatch, boards, reinforcement in blocks and plaster, straw bale construction and geotextiles (for soil stabilization). Carpets made from a natural plastic derived from maize starch, a biopolymer called PLA (poly-lactic acid), have now also entered the market.

Insulation can be made from 100 per cent recycled newsprint. It is said to be more efficient than traditional insulation materials, uses far less energy than glass fibre to make and does not constitute a waste hazard when it is finally disposed of. Flax is also used as an insulating material, using waste fibres from the linen industry as well as virgin fibres. It can be produced using a mechanical process and offcuts can be fed back into the production process. In this way no chemicals are used and no waste is created. Every kilogram of flax used in buildings instead of mineral wool saves around 1.5 kilograms of carbon dioxide emissions.

Board Rigid insulation board and render carrier (indoors and outdoors) can be made from reeds tightly bound using zinc wire. This material works well as part of a 'breathing' wall construction. Wood fibre boards, made by compressing chips of wood at high temperatures and containing no glue or preservatives, can be used to insulate roofs, floors and walls. The chips are a by-product of the timber industry.

Blocks A revolutionary Swiss technology has provided a means for fast construction using hollow timber blocks. Two people can put together an attractive two-storey house in just three days, complete with internal and external walls, cellar, attic and roof. The large hollow

timber blocks slot together without glue or other fixings to form load-bearing internal or external walls. The gaps can house electrical cables and then be filled with insulation. They are made from offcuts of timber from rapidly renewable sources.

Blocks made from clay, straw and timber also are available and provide an environmentally benign modular walling system. They are free from fossil fuel by-products, can be recycled and have low embodied energy.

Cement and concrete

In 1994 as much as 5 per cent of global greenhouse gas production by human activity originated from cement production. About 60 million tonnes of rice hulls (the papery covering over rice grains) are burnt every year, but a pilot plant study has shown that rice producers can burn this waste to produce power while using the ash as a performance-enhancing additive to concrete. Hydrated hydraulic lime can also be used, and its manufacture requires less energy than cement. Shiv, the short fibres from the centre of the hemp stem, can be mixed with a variety of lime mixes to create a solid composite walling material that provides insulation and some structural strength. It is normally cast like concrete in timber shuttering around a timber structural frame and then plastered with lime and sand. A lime mixture has been used in France for years. Now precast hemp and lime blocks are about to go into production in the UK, offering another form of construction.

Green buildings

In 2001 a government survey reported that an estimated 93.91 million tonnes of waste were produced by the construction and demolition industry in England and Wales. In addition to reusing and recycling material, the industry is

Imported straw from Turkey is sometimes used for traditional thatching in the UK

Eden's upper bus shelter is built of traditional cob

Cob building

Traditionally buildings have been made out of materials found in the surrounding landscape including the earth itself. Buildings made from unbaked earth include the adobe houses in North America and the cob houses common in the seventeenth and eighteenth centuries in south-west England. Cob is

a mixture of earth, clay, sand, straw and water, the word 'cob' being old English for a lump or a round mass. Thick cob walls provide excellent thermal insulation. Building with cob is energy-efficient and ecologically sound, representing one of the few natural building methods still employed in England. The clay used for the cob-built public toilet and bus shelter at Eden came from waste materials, and the windows from recycled washing-machine doors. Power for heat and light comes from solar and photovoltaic panels and a windmill.

189

A modern house made of blocks of hemp in Haverhill, Suffolk

looking to reduce the amount of waste generated. Several organizations including the Buildings Research Establishment have also been looking at the environmental impact of construction materials. The materials are being assessed over their entire life cycle, from the extraction of raw materials, through their processing, construction, use and maintenance, to their eventual demolition and disposal. In the UK, the Green Building Challenge was established to develop an internationally agreed framework for the assessment of the environmental impact of buildings. When considering the sustainability of building materials, 'green' architects aim for an almost zero impact on the environment by using renewable and biodegradable materials with low fossil-fuel requirements.

A house of dried mud in Mali

The tropical regions

Throughout the tropics, plants have been used in construction for centuries. In traditional houses, timber forms the basic structure, and branches, stems, leaves and fibres of locally available plants can be used for the roofs, flooring and walls.

Timber

Key tropical timber species include: mahogany (*Swietenia macrophylla*, *S. mahogoni*), native to central America; teak, native to India and South-east Asia; and Gabon-mahogany (*Aucoumea klaineana*), native to Gabon and the Congo. These and other tropical hardwoods are valued for their strength and flexibility, their stability in fluctuating atmospheres and, with certain species, their natural resistance to termite attack. Most of the wood harvested in many tropical forests is used locally.

Of the 8,000-plus tree species that exist relatively few are used in the international timber industry. Only 6 per cent of tropical timber reaches the global trade market legally. Of this, Britain, the second-highest importer in Europe after the Netherlands, imports 8 per cent. In Europe, tropical hardwoods are used as floorings, fittings and furniture, and also, because of their strength, to replace steel in concrete structures in industrial buildings. In the Netherlands tropical hardwoods have been used as flood defences.

The few species we do use for timber are becoming endangered, and even those we do not use become casualties in the extraction process. In response to the increased demand for certified wood, some believe that with effective management timber can be used as a renewable resource.

Teak logging in Java

Malaysian Rumah Kampong village house

The contemporary Asian house in the Humid Tropics Biome at Eden was made from locally available timber, rattan and bamboo. It was constructed by local craftsman who have built houses in South-east Asia and joined by timber frame and bamboo specialists.

Others think that effective management will only tackle the tip of the iceberg. In the tropics logging profits aren't huge and many contracts are short term, so companies aren't willing to invest in long-term sustainability. Large-scale mining projects, intensive agriculture and illegal logging are amongst the activities that have devastating impacts on the world's forests. Also a threat is the domestic use of tropical timber for construction, firewood, crafts and agriculture.

During the last decade the global rate of deforestation has been estimated at around 15 million hectares per annum – equivalent to the area of England and Wales. Up to 80 per cent of logging in tropical forests is illegal, with Britain importing more illegal tropical timber than any other European country. In 2002 thousands of metres of picture frames made from protected ramin worth £130,000 were impounded, the largest seizure of illegal wood products ever seen in Britain.

Ways forward include research into using different timber species; involving forest dwellers in the decision-making process; and developing sustainable livelihoods from non-timber forest products that can be harvested without harming the forest (see page 55).

The African rondavel

The African rondavel provides temporary accommodation for farmers while they tend their cattle and/or crops. It contains the bare essentials: shelter, a sleeping area, a fireplace and a storage place. The rondavel at Eden was constructed by a Cornish archaeologist and the Eden team with advice from our partners in Cameroon. The frame was made of bent wooden branches covered with a cob-like mixture. Raffia was used for the roof.

Bamboo

Bamboo is one of the most versatile plants on Earth, useful for its lightweight strength, which comes from its hollow stems, for its ease of working and for its simple beauty. It is used by half the world's people in thousands of products from huge skyscraper scaffolding to tiny gramophone needles and from slide rules to skins of aeroplanes. It can be used to start a cooking fire in a wet rainforest and its ashes can be used to polish jewels and manufacture electric batteries. It has made bicycles, windmills, musical instruments, paper, strong walls that resist flood and tide, and bridges up to 260 metres long. Bamboo is suited to low-technology processing, as well as industrial manufacturing techniques, and its uses span the world.

Bamboo is an ideal building material for low-cost, low-impact, earthquake-resistant housing projects. Within its walls short, tough fibres sit in a resilient softer matrix providing nature's version of fibreglass. It has great tensile strength, splits straight and is very hard. You can grow your own house from bamboo every five years – bamboo begins growing again immediately after harvesting. In Bangladesh 75 per cent of houses are built from bamboo. When an earthquake shook Colombia's coffee region vast areas of housing collapsed. Nearly all of the five hundred people who died were killed by falling concrete. At the end of those terrible few minutes, many bamboo houses were still standing. In the Humid Tropics Biome at Eden, Housings and Hazards, a company that works with partners to make safer, hazard-resistant housing available and affordable to vulnerable rural communities around the

Bamboo can be used both as a construction material and as scaffolding

193

Bamboo facts

The distribution of bamboo ranges from 50°N of Sakhalin in north Japan to 47°S in Chile. It occurs in altitudes up to 4,000 metres from the warm humid tropics to the cold areas of northern Japan.

Bamboo, a primitive grass, grew on Earth 200 million years ago and will probably outlive us all. At Hiroshima, it survived closer to ground zero than any other living thing. The plant itself can survive conditions from extreme drought to 6 metres of rainfall. There are over a thousand species of bamboo, growing in a variety of forms from tiny dwarfs to towering tropical giants. The tropical giant bamboo (Dendrocalamus asper) *is the fastest growing plant on the planet, recorded growing 1.2 metres skywards in twenty-four hours.*

At certain intervals, sometimes as rarely as once every few hundred years, all bamboos of a given kind, even huge stands from rhizomes transported to far-off lands generations before, flower together all around the world and then die.

Bamboo also has an important role in protecting the earth, binding topsoil in areas of instability where land is eroding, and helping to prevent flooding.

I Ching, The Book of Change, *one of the oldest books in the world, is written on bamboo tablets.*

In Japan people grow square bamboo poles by placing a square wooden mould over the shoots as they grow.

world, have built a bamboo house based on an original design by Simon Velez, an internationally renowned Colombian architect.

Bamboo supports the livelihoods of millions of people worldwide. Much bamboo is still wild harvested but in some areas conservation orders have prevented people from cutting bamboo to make a living. Concern about over-exploitation has led to more focused research on bamboo use and development. IPGRI (the International Plant Genetic Resources Institute), the International Network for Bamboo and Rattan and the United Nations Food and Agriculture Organization are combining genetic-resource activities with research on socio-economic and production aspects.

The Integrated Rural Bamboo project aims to help make bamboo a more useful crop for farmers, artisans, traders and people throughout the developing world (mainly India, but also Indonesia and Bangladesh). Models are being developed for the conservation, increased cultivation and use of rural bamboo. Bringing

'A cup is made
Of bottom and sides
But its use lies in its emptiness.'

Lao Tzu

together diverse groups such as small farmers, weavers, architects, designers, natural scientists, community workers and rural sociologists, the project is increasing the profile of bamboo as a crop for poverty alleviation and environmental protection.

Bamboo is mainly used where it is grown, with a relatively small amount being exported for flooring and furniture. However, with its hollow tough fibres, it has the potential to be made into plastic when fossil-oil-derived plastic polymers, or materials from traditional forests, become scarce and expensive. The story of the rich cultural links between man and bamboo and new sustainability initiatives around the world will help to focus attention on the importance of the past in shaping the future.

The frame of the bamboo house in the Humid Tropics Biome

Palms

In the tropics the diverse forms of the many palm species have traditionally supplied people with far more than oil: building materials, food, fuel, medicine, tools, toys and many other material needs are met by these plants. Here's a brief selection (see also page 41):

Attalea cohune The Cohune palm, from Central America and the north of South America, is used mainly for its fruit kernel oil. Its leaves, up to 10 metres long, are ideal for thatch, and the trunks are used for construction.

Bismarckia nobilis The Bismark palm comes from the drier parts of Madagascar. The trunk is used whole or split for house construction, and the leaves for thatch.

Hyphaene benguelensis This palm is from Africa, Madagascar, the Middle East and India. The fronds are used for thatch and weaving. The hard seeds are carved as vegetable ivory.

A palm house in the Amazon forest, Brazil

Johannesteijsmannia magnifica From South-east Asia, this palm has huge undivided leaves, which make great thatch, shelters and instant umbrellas.

Euterpe oleracea, E. edulis The assai from central South America, through Brazil to Peru, provides an edible heart, and the hard outer part of the stem may be used as planks, and the leaves for thatch.

Calamus inermis, C. deeratus, C. caesius These spiky climbing rattan palms from Asia have inner stems that can be made into furniture, walking sticks, mats and twine. Rattans can provide a wild harvest crop for local people, but demand means that in places the stems are being harvested faster than they can regrow. Research is exploring sustainable production techniques.

Caryota maxima The timber of this palm from India and Sri Lanka is used for construction purposes and the durable leaf sheath fibres for thatch cordage. The woolly coating on the leaf is used as tinder or wadding.

Coconut palm in Borneo

Cocos nucifera Coconuts from the coastal tropics of the world produce far more than a tasty snack. Coir from the husk makes ropes, mats, mattresses, brushes and potting compost. Coir dust makes insulation, plasterboard and house bricks. Coconut shells make cups, pots, buckles and charcoal (once mixed with egg white to make black, shiny, very hard floors). The white flesh, copra, provides oil for soap, candles, hair conditioners and even toothpaste. The leaves are used as thatch, mats, screens, hats and baskets. The leaf sheaths make bags and slippers.

Stripping coir from coconuts in Peru

Rubber

For centuries the Olmecs, the Mayans and the Aztecs of Mexico and the Incas of Peru used the latex from the *Hevea brasiliensis* tree to produce rubber. European demand for this flexible natural product took the tree to pastures new.

The fathers of the Western rubber industry were Charles de la Condamine, who studied rubber during his explorations of Peru in 1735, and François Fresneau, who first documented rubber's unusual elastic properties. In the 1770s Joseph Priestley popularized the use of rubber for erasing pencil writing (which is how it got its name).

From farmers to plantations

As the demand for rubber grew in the nineteenth century, the issue of Amerindian slavery and the scarcity of skilled labour meant that natural rubber from the wild rainforests of South America became increasingly hard to find. In

Part of the Rubber exhibit at Eden

1876 the British botanist Henry Wickham collected seventy thousand rubber-tree seeds from Brazil and sent them to the Royal Botanic Gardens at Kew.

Nineteen hundred of the seventy thousand seeds at Kew germinated and the seedlings were exported to Sri Lanka. A year later, in 1877, twenty-five seedlings were transferred from Sri Lanka to Singapore. From Singapore the seedlings travelled onwards to Malaysia, where the rubber industry became established. Nearly all the rubber trees in the Far East come from these twenty-five seedlings.

Today over three-quarters of rubber is synthetic. The rapid replacement of natural with synthetic rubber was largely due to the two world wars, which limited the rubber supply and spurred Germany and America to invent a synthetic alternative. After a rise in the price of crude oil and the arrival of AIDS, natural rubber began to make a bit of a comeback, partly for condoms and rubber gloves. Each day 50 million rubber latex gloves are used worldwide.

Thailand continues to be the largest rubber exporter, producing over 1.6 million tonnes per year. Yet while Far Eastern countries have hugely benefited from the rubber industry, Malaysia and Thailand in particular have lost thousands of hectares of rainforest to rubber plantations. In contrast, Brazil, the source of rubber, still holds some of the largest blocks of undisturbed rainforest, but its original rubber industry is virtually extinct. Today some rubber is being sourced from smallholdings and 'extractive rainforest reserves' rather than plantations.

In the rubber industry today sustainability is a major challenge. Over three-quarters of all natural rubber goes into making tyres. In 1910 this was a mere 2.5 million tyres, but by 1990 this figure had risen to 860 million worldwide. In Britain over 40 million tyres were wasted in 1999, and until only recently most tyres went into landfill sites (the next biggest contributor after nappies). Thanks to a range of projects, over 70 per cent of all tyres are now recycled and reused.

Rubbery facts

In the USA latex protein allergy is a recent and growing problem. Between the 1930s and 1980s rubber was used in a wide range of products, from baby's bottle teats to gloves and condoms, and experts now suggest that this excessive use of rubber has led to this allergy.

One of the key success factors that underpinned the expansion of the Malaysian rubber industry was a tapping technique that did not require the tree to be felled or to die after extraction.

In the Second World War the Japanese took control of 95 per cent of the rubber plantations. In response, the USA banned the use of all non-essential items, reduced the speed limit to 35 mph to reduce wear on tyres, and introduced a massive rubber-recycling scheme.

As to the future: researchers are working on producing albumin from rubber-tree latex. This is the protein in human blood given in transfusions. In time the by-product of the industry could be the rubber!

199

Plant fibres

Plants are made up of cellulose, lignin, sugars, starch and water. The fibrous parts are high in cellulose, a stiff, strong natural polymer. Linked together, polymer chains act like steel hawsers, taking the load of wind and weight. We use these fibres for our own ends to make things such as cotton clothing and jute twine.

Cotton

Cotton (*Gossypium* spp.) is the world's biggest non-food crop, and makes half the world's textiles. Most cotton is grown by smallholders in developing countries, but 70 per cent of cotton

exports come from the USA, the second-biggest producer after China. Versatile and durable, cotton has survived competition from synthetics, but at the expense of heavy fertilizer, pesticide and defoliant use as well as a long history of labour exploitation. It is estimated that over 20 per cent of the world's pesticides are used on cotton.

Naturally coloured cottons were grown up to five thousand years ago in the Indian sub-continent, Egypt and Peru. With the Industrial Revolution white cotton gained favour because it could be dyed any colour. Today growers are considering producing organic naturally coloured types again, partly to avoid the use of toxic dyes.

Picking cotton by hand in Peru

Long cotton fibres are spun into thread for textiles, towelling, paper, banknotes, fishing nets, tents, nappies, wallpaper, bandages, surgical sutures, rope and sheets. The short fibres, or linters, provide cellulose used for dynamite, sausage skins, lino, cellophane, rayon, photographic film, nail polish, moulded plastic and solid fuel rockets, and to thicken ice cream, make chewing gum chewy and allow make-up to flow smoothly. Crushed seed yields a useful vegetable oil and the meal from the crushed seeds is used for cattle feed, fish bait and organic fertilizer.

Every year, cotton is grown on 33 million hectares, equivalent to about one and a half times Britain's total land area. If we grew all the cotton we use in Britain, it would need a fifth of our farmland. Cotton can be seen as an environmental and social villain, but it is also a vital source of livelihood, employment and economic development for growers. Expanding demand for organic cotton, at present around 1 per cent of the harvest, is also beginning to change the industry.

Organic cotton

The Eden Project Store is linked to Agrocel, a company that makes organic, fairly traded products in northern India.

- *Farmers deal directly with the company, not middlemen.*
- *Agrocel provides technical and agricultural advice for local farmers.*
- *The company's practices are audited.*
- *Product sales include a donation for education and medical care.*

Jute

Although cloth made from jute (*Corchorus capsularis*) was widely known to the British in India, it was regarded as inferior 'native cloth' of no intrinsic export value to the rest of the Empire until Napoleon blockaded the Baltic ports, cutting off Britain's supply of flax and hemp from Russia through Estonia, Latvia and Lithuania. After the Napoleonic Wars, jute was used for a number of domestic products such as sacking, carpet backing and twine. The industry boomed until the 1950s when synthetic fibres began to replace all natural fibres. Nylon filament replaced twine; polyethylene became a cheaper alternative carpet backing; and polythene bags replaced sacking.

Jute is still used as a backing material on linoleum. Chemical treatment of jute by acetylation can transform a naturally water-absorbent fibre into a hydrophobic one that takes up oils more readily. This treated fibre can be used to mop up oil slicks. Acetylation of plant fibre matting can also improve the resin penetration and strength of biocomposite panels.

Flax

Called *Linum usitatissimum* by the Romans – literally 'most useful flax' – flax (pictured left) has provided seed oil for inks, paints and varnishes, animal feed from the crushed seed residue and,

most importantly, fine long fibres to produce linen. In Egyptian times linen was regarded as a 'royal cloth', used to wrap mummies. The Romans took flax across Europe, where it adapted to climates from Scandinavia to Spain. The small seed was easily packed and provided a high-protein food and herbal medicine for travellers, and, once cultivated and harvested, the long fibres would be spun for use as weaving yarns, fishing line and nets as well as twine and rope.

Linen is valued for its comfort next to the skin in hot climates, the result of its high moisture absorbency and heat-conducting properties. It fell out of favour after the 1950s with the introduction of synthetic fibres but new spinning techniques, including blending with cotton or ramie, have lowered prices and produced more easily laundered fabrics.

By 2000 the European automotive industry was using almost 25,000 tonnes of flax and another 10,000 tonnes of other plant fibres such as coir, jute and hemp a year, mainly in the construction of interior door panels and parcel shelves. The future of the crop is dependent on its profitability for the farmer and industrialist.

Sisal

Native to Central America, the fibrous leaves of sisal (*Agave sisalana*) were used by Mexicans for

Sisal drying in Mexico

centuries before the Spanish conquistadors arrived. Spanish seamen quickly appreciated its superior qualities when made into marine rope, which was not only as tough and strong as their European hemp ropes but more resistant to salt-water rotting. It was cultivated in many parts of the world, but was found most suited to commercial production in Ecuador and Tanzania.

Today the bulk of sisal is used as agricultural baler twine for straw and hay bales. Although polypropylene twine is used on European farms, American farmers have always preferred sisal twine because of its biodegradability. A revival of sisal in agriculture in the European Union (EU) is predicted, prompted by legislation on pollution by plastic in the environment. Current EU policy encourages farmers to care for the rural environment for everyone's benefit, not just to produce cheap food using the cheapest materials. A resurgence in the use of sisal as twine and rope would also be a huge benefit for farmers in Africa and Central and Southern America.

Abaca

When Portuguese sailors landed in Manila (in the Philippines), the similarity of the local ropes to their own European hemp ropes led them to name the fibre 'Manila hemp'. Decades later botanists classified this fibre, abaca, as *Musa textilis*, a species of the banana plant. This fibre has similar wet-strength properties to sisal and makes an even stronger rope.

Ropes were replaced when ships came into dock and the old ropes were sold for cash, resulting in the expression 'money for old rope'. The pulped ropes were made into the strong brown envelopes known as 'manila'. The term remains in stationery catalogues, although the modern brown-paper envelope is made from unbleached wood pulp. In some countries tea bags are still made from manila.

Musa textilis could well provide a good supply of raw fibre today, as well as a much-needed boost to the rural economy of the Philippines, to meet the need for new forms of

This hemp may eventually be used for soundproofing Mercedes car doors

paper-based products. In the Philippines fine white gauze-like embroidered clothes are still made from abaca.

Bashofu

The hardy Japanese banana (*Musa basjoo*) grown by keen gardeners is the source of fibre for a rare fabric, bashofu, used in Okinawa, Japan, for making kimonos.

Hemp

Few plants in history have been such constant companions to so many civilizations as hemp (*Cannabis sativa*) has, and few plants have produced two such radically different products. Originally from the Indian subcontinent, it spread from China to France and from Russia to Africa. As with flax, the seed can be used as a food protein and the outer stem provides fibre for ropes and canvas for tents. Unlike flax, the leaves can be dried and smoked to provide a

mild narcotic. Hemp growing became common-place in Britain under the Romans and continued into the mid-1940s.

Concern over new strains of high-THC (delta9-tetrahydrocannabinol) cannabis being over-used as a recreational drug led law enforcement agencies in many parts of the world to press for legislation to control its use. In England 6,000 hectares of low-THC hemp is now grown for fibre under Home Office drug licence and supervision. In Scotland, a high-THC crop is grown under secure glasshouse conditions and under the same drug licence, and is being used in the development of a pharmacological muscle relaxant for multiple-sclerosis sufferers. The fibre crop in Europe is today mostly grown to supply the specialist paper industry, or for the non-woven converting industry supplying automotive companies. The outlook for hemp is bright. Like flax, it provides a good break crop for the farmer, giving the land a rest from other crops and helping to prevent disease. Unlike flax, it does not require the same level of fertilizer or indeed any post-emergent agro-chemicals. It is naturally resilient to most pests and diseases and tolerates most soil types.

Hemp growing in the outside display at Eden

New Zealand flax

When Captain James Cook, the great navigator, and Joseph Banks, the great botanist, arrived in New Zealand in 1769, they noticed the native Maori people wearing a fine cloth similar to linen and as a result this became known as New Zealand flax. Botanically, however, *Phormium tenax* is slow-growing and low-yielding, and the fibre is comparable in quality to jute rather than flax in that it is dull, weak and coarse. Despite attempts to set up plantations and processing factories in many temperate parts of the world including South Africa and the island of St Helena in the South Atlantic, as well as its native New Zealand, none has survived – although in St Helena it has become an invasive weed. New Zealand flax is the Cinderella of fibres, waiting for a Prince Charming to recognize its potential for some exciting new application.

Milkweed

Milkweed (*Asclepias* spp.) produces two distinctly different fibres from the same plant. A fine protective white floss-fibre covers the seed and this has been used for centuries throughout Europe as a good filling for pillows and quilts. It is light as goose down, has insulating proper-ties and, being hydrophobic, is less inclined to rot and smell than some other fibres. The stem of the plant, which can grow over 1 metre high, can be harvested and processed like flax or hemp. The yield is very low, however, and if the bolls (seed capsules) are not harvested at the right time the fibres are scattered by the wind.

Nettles

'Grasp the nettle' is a term that perhaps should also be applied to developing a new attitude towards this much-maligned plant (*Urtica dioica*). Our forebears used nettle leaves to make herbal tea, extracted white silk-like fibres from the stem to be spun and woven into fine cloth, and grew the plants on their middens where the prodigious root growth helped turn a smelly mess into compost for use on their cottage gardens. Mary, Queen of Scots, is said to have insisted on nettle sheets, as they were finer and softer than the coarse linens used for bedding in her time. Napoleon's army is thought to have worn nettle clothes. In the First World War they were used to make sandbags, rucksacks and harnesses, and, in the Second World War, parachutes.

Farmers, who once eradicated this pernicious weed wherever possible, are starting to take an interest in growing it. As well as being a potentially valuable fibre crop, nettles also provide a wildlife habitat for butterflies and voles. Recently De Montfort University has launched a project called Sustainable Technologies in Nettle Growing (STING) aimed at producing nettle fabrics. The initiative is partly to find crops other than food for farmers to grow and partly to reduce our reliance on cotton, which is not generally environmentally friendly (see page 200) (in reality this is a very long-term option). Italian fashion houses already have nettle products, including jeans, on the catwalk and Japanese fashion buyers are purchasing nettle fibres too.

Nettles

Paper

Paper can be strong or delicate, permanent or temporary, and even though it decomposes in water, it can be made into umbrellas and boats. Produced from renewable materials and with the potential to be recycled, paper seems to be a non-polluting sustainable resource. Yet its manufacture is one of the most hotly debated environmental issues of all.

Ninety-five per cent of paper is made from the wood of 40 out of a possible 20,000 tree species. Research is being carried out into disease-resistant, fast-growing and even genetically modified trees in order to increase supply. The industry is also considering the use of herbaceous plants such as hemp and flax in paper manufacture to take the pressure off the forests.

Reeds are an ancient source of paper fibre

Eight thousand years to perfect paper

The word 'paper' comes from 'papyrus' (*Cyperus papyrus*), the plant the Egyptians used as a writing material over six thousand years ago. Paper as we know it today originated in China however, in AD 100, when mulberry bark, hemp and rags were pulped and dried in sheets.

The first British paper mill, built in 1488, used old clothes and rags for pulp. By the 1700s, demand for paper had outstripped supply and a new raw material was needed. The answer to the problem came from the wasp when it was noticed that its papery nests were made from chewed-up wood. The principles are the same in modern paper manufacture. Mashing up woody

How much paper do we use?

Do we use too much paper? It all depends where we live. Today 25 per cent of the world's population consumes 75 per cent of the world's paper. In the move towards sustainable paper production, environmental as well as economic issues need to be considered.

- *Total world annual consumption of paper is approximately 270 million tonnes (58 per cent from wood pulp, 4 per cent from non-wood pulp, 38 per cent from waste paper).*
- *Pulp and paper production is predicted to increase to 396 million tonnes by 2010.*
- *The paper industry accounts for about 2 per cent of world trade.*
- *Britain is the world's fifth-highest consumer of paper. Each of us consumes on average 189 kilograms of paper and board a year.*
- *In Britain we get through 2.2 million tonnes of newsprint every year.*
- *In the world 1.2 billion letters are sent through the post every day.*
- *272 million trees, about one per person, are felled in the USA each year to produce newspapers and magazines.*

material into a pulp removes the sticky substances that hold the cellulose fibres in place and the remaining fibrous mass can be made into any shape or form, be it a nest or a sheet of paper.

In the early 1800s the first practical paper-making machine was developed in Britain, producing paper in a continuous sheet. Chemical pulping began to take over from the mechanical process. Sulphate pulp, known as 'kraft' after the German word for strength, now accounts for around 70 per cent of all wood-pulp manufacture.

In forestry plantations and working forests concerns have been raised about loss of biodiversity, soil erosion, loss of soil fertility, watershed destabilization, reduced access for local people, reduced local control of land and displacement of rural communities. Forest management is changing, however. The trend is away from exploitative approaches and towards a sustainable system where forest management mimics natural forest, thereby protecting the ecosystem. Today there is also a greater reliance on plantations and intensively managed forest that can help to conserve original natural forest.

Paper mill effluents are relatively benign, the pulping stage being the main source of the industry's pollutants. Advances in technology have resulted in some improvements in pulping, including lower water consumption and increasing use of biomass fuels (see page 219). Pollution by emissions is also being addressed following concerns about the use of chlorine in the bleaching process.

Waste paper

Waste paper can be put into landfill, incinerated, composted, recycled or reused.

- Each tonne of landfill paper takes up 3 cubic metres and produces methane, which is twenty-five times more potent than carbon dioxide as a greenhouse gas. Capturing the methane could help this problem.

- Incineration is becoming much cleaner and more efficient in terms of energy conversion, providing an alternative to recycling paper that is too costly to separate from other waste.
- Paper can be combined with biowaste in composting, an important option when there is insufficient paper to justify incineration.
- Recycling reduces landfill waste. Paper can be recycled between five and eight times before the plant fibres it contains become too short to use. Recycling relieves pressure on forests, provides employment opportunities and uses less total energy than the production of virgin paper. The BioRegional Development organization has developed a mill with Chinese partners suitable for urban recycling of waste paper with hemp fibres added for strength.

Kenaf (from Hibiscus annabinus) provides a possible new fibre source for the paper industry

Blue, yellow, red, orange

Dye plants have been used worldwide for thousands of years. In our temperate climate, woad (*Isatis tinctoria*) (blue), weld (*Reseda luteola*) (yellow) and madder (*Rubia tinctorum*) (red) make up the triumvirate of British dye plants. In subtropical and tropical climates indigo (*Indigofera tinctoria*) yields the same blue dye as woad, and annatto (*Bixa orellana*) colours our cheese orange and sweets red. In the warm temperate regions grows saffron (*Crocus sativus*), used to dye the robes of Buddhist monks, and sunflowers (*Helianthus* spp.), used by the Hopi Indians to produce a purple-black dye.

Blue dye

Natural indigo is found in several very different plant species across the world. Nevertheless, synthetic indigo now supplies most of our needs. But new technology means that natural, renewable, non-toxic indigo from European woad plants and from subtropical indigo plants may well be able to compete economically with synthetics.

Indigo's unique chemistry demands an extraction process that approaches alchemy. The chemical in the plants that makes indigo is colourless and the blue dye does not appear until the leaves are processed. One way is to heat them in water with a touch of lime. The mixture has to be vigorously whisked, to add oxygen, until a blue foam appears on the surface, showing that the invisible indoxyl chemical has oxidized to indigo.

The extracted indigo dye is insoluble – not the most useful attribute for a dye! It has to be

Vietnamese Black Hamong people dye their clothes with indigo

put in the dye vat and chemically 'reduced' to a soluble yellow chemical, called leuco-indigo, partially achieved by removing oxygen from the mixture. Cloth is then gently lowered into the vat. It emerges yellow but as it comes into contact with the air it changes – to a beautiful blue, for ever.

Yellow dye

Weld (*Reseda luteola*) is a biennial herb that produces a rosette of long narrow leaves one year and tall flowering spikes with numerous small yellow flowers the next. Also known as dyer's rocket, the plant is native to Europe and south-west Asia but can now also be found throughout western Asia and North Africa. All parts of the plant except the roots contain the strong bright yellow pigment luteolin.

Weld has been a popular source of yellow colouring for three thousand years, the Romans using it to dye the robes of vestal virgins. Like so many dyes, in the twentieth century it was replaced by cheaper synthetic alternatives.

With the recent revival of interest in natural dyes, researchers have been looking into the optimum conditions for cultivating and harvesting weld in order to assess its suitability as a dye crop.

Red dye

Madder (*Rubia tinctorum*) is native to western and central Asia and has become naturalized in much of central and southern Europe. Until the middle of the nineteenth century it was one of the most popular dye plants, cultivated for its long fleshy roots from which a brilliant red pigment was extracted. The invention of cheaper synthetic alizarin in 1868, the first synthetic substitute for a vegetable dye, caused a rapid decline in madder cultivation.

Flax textiles were dyed with madder in Egypt in 1370 BC, and dyed cotton textiles from the

Indigo, the world's oldest dye

- *Indigo accompanied Egyptian mummies to the next world and the ancient Britons into battle.*
- *It was the 'blue spice' that travelled the trade routes from East to West.*
- *It coloured frescos, early wall paintings and the vessels of the Dead Sea Scrolls.*
- *It made the sixteenth-century European woad merchants rich and famous.*
- *Gandhi supported the political unrest of the indigo workers, which was one of the factors that led to demands for Indian independence.*
- *Indigo caused conflicts such as the 'woad wars' at the end of the Middle Ages and the rows in Britain's parliament between the opium and indigo growers in Bengal.*
- *It never fades.*

Indus region have been dated to around 3000 BC. Madder has been found in Egyptian tombs, is referred to in the Bible, and was prized by the ancient Greeks and Romans. By the first millennium BC it was used extensively throughout the Middle East and Mediterranean basin to colour linen, cotton, wool and leather. It grew in importance in Europe in the Middle Ages and was grown extensively in France and Germany, but the highest-quality madder came from Turkey, Holland and France. The Dutch monopolized production from the sixteenth to eighteenth centuries, even exporting it to India.

The plant has been used as a medicinal herb throughout history. Its high tannin content makes it beneficial for intestinal problems, acting as an antibiotic and anti-inflammatory. It has also been used to treat amenorrhoea (failure to menstruate) and to break up kidney stones.

The main problem in cultivating madder for

Extracting red dye in Amazonia

dye is that the roots are extremely brittle and mechanical extraction breaks them. By using existing cultivation, harvesting and processing technology, however, production is feasible, although labour-intensive. But when producing it, as with most natural dyes it is difficult to give assurances of quality, standardization of plant material and fastness of colour.

Orange dye

Turmeric, the bright orange powder from *Curcuma longa* gives a rich but fugitive dye. The yellow spots on fashionable nineteenth-century silk bandanas came from turmeric. The spots used to turn red when washed with soap, returning to yellow after rinsing and drying. At that time it was mainly used, with other dyes, to make browns and olive greens. Today it colours our curries and cakes.

Traditionally saffron dye is used to colour monks' robes

Tomorrow's technologies

There is nothing new about the use of renewable plant materials for industrial production. Henry Ford, for example, built a car out of hemp-based composite material fuelled with hemp oil, and a flax-reinforced biocomposite Spitfire fuselage was built in the 1940s. Early lubricants were based on oil extracted from castor oil plant seeds (*Ricinus communis*). Castor seed oil gained a reputation as a lubricant for high-performance racing motorbikes – a purpose for which it is still used today. From the 1940s onwards, petrochemical-based industry became predominant. In recent years, however, there has been a revival of interest in the growth and use of renewable industrial crops in Europe.

Bioplastics

The British use about eight billion plastic bags a year, the majority of which end up in landfill sites. Now, however, plant-based plastics offer a biodegradable alternative. Starch (typically from maize, wheat or potatoes) is sometimes at the start of the process for making these bioplastics. Alternatively plant sugars (from maize or sugar beet, for example) are fermented by bacteria to make poly-lactic acid, another starting point for bioplastics.

A consequence of our modern fast-food society is rubbish bins full of polystyrene

Biodegradable plastic cutlery

containers used for take-away food. Some bioplastic manufacturers are making containers that look and behave like polystyrene but that biodegrade after about a month. A Dutch firm is turning potato peelings into starch granules, which are used to make biodegradable potato-plastic plant pots. For society to benefit from these new, biodegradable materials, the establishment of more municipal composting sites is a priority. As far as waste management is concerned, either at the local council or household level, the UK is a long way behind the rest of Europe.

There are several factors that will affect the success of bioplastics over conventional petrochemical-based plastics: cost, sustainability and performance. Various factors can influence cost, including legislation and green taxes. Taxation on plastic bags, such as that introduced by the Irish government, is one way of preventing our limited landfill sites filling up so quickly with plastic, which does not rot. Recent legislation in Europe has been drafted under which conventional plastic pots used for raising plants are classified as waste and will incur a waste tax, favouring recycling and the use of pots made of renewable plant-based plastics.

In 2001 fewer than 0.1 per cent of the world's plastics were made from biologically based renewable materials. This will change if there is sufficient demand.

Specialist oils

Oilseed rape (*Brassica napus*), sunflower oil (*Helianthus* spp.) and soya oil (*Glycine* spp.) can all be used to make lubricant and specialist oils. Plant oils have limitations in terms of performance, compared with mineral oils, but these problems are being overcome by a combination of chemistry and breeding. For example, new varieties of oilseed rape and sunflower high in oleic acid are being bred. Rapeseed and crambe (*Crambe abyssinica*), high in erucic acid, produce a substance that is used as a 'slip agent', allowing plastic carrier bags to be opened more easily. It is also used in specialist heatproof inks used on till receipts. In Belgium soya-based printing inks are used for most of the country's

Oilseed rape in China

214

Tomorrow's plants

Maize (Zea mays) [right] Maize starch makes plastics for biodegradable packaging, cutlery, carrier bags, nappies and tyres.

Crambe (Crambe abyssinica) Crambe oil helps open supermarket bags, forms part of the ink in till receipts and acts as a machinery lubricant.

Sunflower (Helianthus annuus) [left] provides pollution-free chainsaw lubricants and plant plastic food trays.

Viper's bugloss (Echium vulgare) Echium oil, rich in fatty acids, can be used as an ingredient in anti-ageing skin creams.

Gold of pleasure (Camelina sativa) provides oils used in hand creams and balsam tissues to make them soft and prevent sore noses.

Soybean (Glycine max.) [right] products can be used in printing inks, rail grease, combine-harvester plastic body parts, wax crayons, printing inks and hurricane-proof roofs.

Borage (Borago officinalis) [left] Rich in gamma linolenic acid, borage can be used in a range of nutraceutical products as an anti-inflammatory, and for eczema and dermatitis.

Pot marigold (Calendula officinalis) [right] Using marigold oil as a carrying agent in paint avoids the use of volatile organic solvents.

Marigold
Calendula
% Calendula is found in new environmentally friendly paints

newspapers and some of Eden's publications already use vegetable-based inks.

Sometimes specialist plant-based additives have distinct health advantages compared with petrochemical alternative – for instance, that in paint diluent made from pot marigold seed oil. Farmers can now buy tractors that use plant-based hydraulic and transmission lubricants that break down rapidly if spilt on the ground. Many of Eden's work vehicles now use plant-based hydraulic oil.

Biocomposites

Biocomposites are rigid structures formed from resins reinforced with plant fibres. Hemp and flax fibres are particularly popular in Europe. Biocomposites have replaced some glass-reinforced plastic components in cars since the early 1990s. Non-woven plant-fibre mats are cheaper and lighter and reduce the vehicle's weight and its fuel consumption. Biocomposites have recently been developed which can be used for external body panels that are as strong as aluminium.

Research into developing composites and polymers from plant-based materials is taking more and more manufacturing industries in a new direction and at the same time providing a boost to Britain's agriculture. Bio-based composites, where the resin binder is made from plant oils rather than synthetic chemicals, will make these materials totally biodegradable and not toxic.

New legislation aims to ensure that new vehicles contain 85 per cent of recyclable materials by January 2006. This percentage rises to 95 per cent by January 2015, the onus being on the manufacturers to take cars back at the end of their lives for disassembly and disposal. The question here is whether disposing of biocomposite car panels, by burning or composting, can be classed as recycling energy, and whether the carbon dioxide released by burning or rotting will be absorbed by the next generation of industrial crop plants.

Plants for cars

Dr Rudolf Diesel originally designed his engine to run on peanut oil. Recently there has been much interest in biodiesel (see page 219). Car tyres are now available that contain high levels of maize starch, replacing most of the carbon black and making tyres more sustainable as well as more energy-efficient because of their reduced rolling resistance. When we apply our car brakes many of us are relying on the oil made from cashew nut shell liquid, an interesting and inexpensive by-product from the cashew nut industry, which is being used to form the heat-absorbing resin component of brake pads. It is also being investigated as a resin for biocomposite panels. Car manufacture is also benefiting in other ways from biocomposites.

Cashew nuts grow at the tip of fruits

From cradle to cradle

Life-cycle analysis is the study of the physical and environmental cost of a product 'from cradle to grave', although life-cycle analysts now use the term 'from cradle to cradle' to indicate the recyclability of products. The length of life, the end of life, and the energy used in the manufacture and use of a product are all assessed when judging sustainable manufacture. Several European car manufacturers have used life-cycle analysis to compare panels made of conventional glass-reinforced fibre with those made of biocomposite material. Studies have generally favoured the lighter biocomposite panels because they not only reduce the weight of a car and help to save fuel but are easier to dispose of at the end of the car's life.

Producing enough fibre from hemp and flax for a year's production of car parcel shelves requires careful forward planning, as the crop is only harvested once a year. Another issue is price. Value-added by-products could improve the economics of growing these crops. 'Biocascading' is a new term used to describe the series of different uses made of a range of crop components. For example, wheat straw, which was once mainly burnt, is being reassessed as a valuable source of pulp and construction material.

In Eden's Plants for Tomorrow's Industries exhibit (right) a beautiful array of colourful crops acts as a backdrop to an exhibition of the wide range of products that can be derived from them.

Plants for fuel

Energy use is central to human society. Over many thousands of years, most of our fuel has come from plants. The Industrial Revolution brought us coal, a new form of slave, but we are coming to the end of the fossil-fuel age. As resources run low, pollution levels run high and our energy needs continue to rise, we are looking for new alternatives, turning again to plants for help.

In this fast-living age of technology, cars, convenience and commodities have all become a necessity in everyday life. Persuading people to revert to a less mechanized way of life, such as using public transport to commute instead of cars, has been unsuccessful, so it seems that we will continue to consume large quantities of fuel every year. It is known that all forms of energy we use have some sort of negative environmental impact, some more than others; there is no entirely clean type of fuel. What we can do to minimize this impact is to diversify the fuel types that we use and continue to develop alternatives.

Most of all, we can still try to cut down on the amount of fuel we use in the first place.

Energy crops

To provide an additional electricity capacity of 1,500 megawatts, equivalent to 600,000 kettles being switched on at the same time, around 125,000 hectares of energy crops will be needed for burning. Current initiatives to achieve this target include grants for growing high-yielding willow and poplar for short-rotation coppice and elephant grass, but uptake of these grants has been slow. In addition to providing opportunities for using redundant agricultural land, crops such as these may be planted on low-grade land such as landfill sites, mining spoils and contaminated ex-industrial land, helping soil stabilization and bioremediation of contaminated soils.

A commercial oil palm forest in Cameroon

Biomass

Biomass – organic matter used as fuel, especially in the generation of electricity – covers a wide range of materials including trees, plants and associated residues; plant fibre, animal manures and agricultural waste. Burning it is less polluting than fossil-fuel alternatives, it is renewable, recycles waste and provides fertilizer as a by-product. Burning biomass is regarded as carbon neutral as the emissions equal the amount of carbon dioxide absorbed by the plants as they grow, although this balance is dependent on the amount of energy used during production and processing.

People have been burning firewood, charcoal, peat, crop residues and dung for millennia – mostly in a sustainable way. Wood was the key source of fuel until the second half of the nineteenth century when more concentrated fossil fuels were introduced. In developing nations wood and other plant materials are still widely used and in many countries account for three-quarters of the energy consumed.

One of the most important benefits of biomass energy is that it is a low-cost, decentralized technology that works best on a small scale, unlike nuclear or fossil-fuel power. The systems can be installed quickly and cheaply, and local resources remain under local control for the benefit of people in the area. This helps to distribute employment, income and the benefits of regional development more equally. The growing of biomass also provides farmers with an alternative crop.

Before energy crops are grown on a large scale, however, it is important to maximize the use of biofuel resources that are residues, such as forest thinnings, straw and manures, sugar cane bagasse, and sawdust from timber plants. The British government aims to provide 6 per cent of its electricity by using biomass by 2020.

A key criticism of biomass energy is the environmental consequence of putting land into cultivation for fuel plants. It is also important to ensure that we get more energy out than we put in and that we measure the environmental impact of transportation, tractors, harvesting machines, and artificial fertilizers and pesticides. Renewable energy alone may not be able to sustain Western lifestyles for the global population. We need to strive to reduce our energy use as well.

Biodiesel and bioethanol

Some plants, such as oilseed rape, sunflower, soybean and palm, produce oils that can be chemically altered to be compatible with diesel engines, offering an environmentally friendly alternative to petroleum-based fuels. Biodiesel produces similar harmful emissions to those of normal diesel and in fact will actually increase some emissions, but it degrades quickly and causes fewer human health problems.

Bioethanol is produced from the fermentation of plant sugars. A high proportion of vehicles in Brazil are powered by sugar ethanol. In Britain 600,000 tonnes of wheat is grown annually for bioethanol, although it is all exported to Spain and Portugal for conversion and use there.

A car filling up with sugar-ethanol in Brazil

Other future fuels

Solar power

Growing plants to supplement our fuel supply is one option; another option is to copy plants and use the sun. By studying their intricate structure we have tried to replicate their methods of both obtaining and storing fuel. Sunlight is free, is renewable, generates no emissions and is silent.

The natural process of photosynthesis can be imitated in solar panels and in production of hydrogen for fuel cells. To obtain the hydrogen, either the hydrocarbons in fossil fuels are reformed into hydrogen and carbon (but using fossil fuel rather defeats the point) or electrolysis is used to split water into oxygen and hydrogen. The one by-product of electrolysis is water vapour, but the energy produced is only as clean as the process used to create the electricity. Provided renewable energy sources are used, hydrogen fuel could be a clean, efficient and widely available alternative power source, although the costs are still prohibitive. Scientists have known for several decades that plants hold the key to splitting water but have not been able to replicate it cheaply. In early 2004, an international team in Japan made an important advance by using high-resolution X-ray crystallography to make an image of the tiny atomic splitter within plants used in photosynthesis. From this, they have identified the key protein involved, giving a clearer understanding of the structure of the reaction centre. They now hope to design a system to provide what could be one of the most promising energy sources of the future, efficient, low-polluting and mobile.

Biomimicry

By closely examining the way in which natural materials are formed and how natural systems function, we can discover models for new products, systems and processes. Throughout history human beings have found inspiration for technical innovation in nature. Plants are amongst the world's most highly evolved designers. They have, after all, had 400 million years to perfect the art. Sir Joseph Paxton based the design of the Crystal Palace for the Great Exhibition in 1851 on the structure of a lily pad. Today, the development of micro- and even nano-scale analytical studies of plant form has taken botanical biomimicry to another level. Nature may be able to provide some of the solutions to today's complex problems.

The helicopter

Through its natural aerodynamics a sycamore seed uses auto-rotation to create lift, and its whirling flight slows down the speed by which the seed reaches the ground, allowing it to be transported by the wind. Together these attributes allow the seed to be dispersed further afield. Though Leonardo da Vinci is credited with the theoretical invention of the helicopter in the fifteenth century, it was the Chinese who in 400 BC invented a sycamore-inspired toy, a spinning top with feathers, believed to be the first man-made device to achieve vertical flight.

Nano-parachutes

The white feathery tufts of dandelion and thistle seeds decrease the rate that the seeds sink to the ground, enabling them to drift a long way from the plant. Human parachutes work in much the same way. An American/Israeli team of researchers have used this technology and that of tiny insects called thrips to develop nano-sized parachutes that can detect harmful toxins in the

The parachute seeds of dandelions

air. The nano-parachutes are made of fibres that are a thousand times finer than a human hair. The parachutes open when released and the chemical sensors in which they are coated change colour when airborne toxins are present, a facility particularly valuable in the case of chemical or biological attack.

Velcro

Velcro, one of the most-used fasteners today, was inspired by a chance discovery on a nature walk. A Swiss amateur naturalist returned home to find that both he and his dog were covered in small burrs from the burdock plant. Examining

*Burdock (*Arctium lappa*) – the inspiration behind Velcro*

these under a microscope he saw the way in which numerous stiff hooks latched on to the soft fibres of his clothes. Working with a textile weaver, he developed a hook and loop fastener, using nylon sewn under infrared light, to imitate the stiff hooks of the burdock seed.

Responsive clothing

Scientists in Reading University's Bio-mimetics Centre have studied the opening and closing of pine cones to design innovative clothing that allows the release of water vapour according to the wearer's activity. The pine cone remains closed while still on the tree but opens when it has ripened and fallen to the ground, releasing its seeds. The layers of pine cone scales react differently to humidity. When the cone dries out, the scales bend open as one of its layers expands more than the other. The clothing mimics this process in reverse by creating a multi-layered textile with lots of tiny flaps. These automatically open when the wearer starts to perspire, allowing water vapour out and cooling the body, and close when the humidity returns to normal. It is envisaged that the fabric will be useful in the defence industry where a minimum amount of clothing is preferable. So, for example, a soldier in the desert could wear the same clothing during the baking daytime heat and the freezing night.

Self-cleaning spray

Lotus leaves are covered in tiny particles, thousandths of a millimetre high, that are coated in a waxy film. Because of these, when water droplets meet the leaf surface they do so at only a few points and roll off easily, propelled by their own weight, gathering dirt as they go. A German botanist has patented a self-cleaning spray based on this concept. When applied to a range of surfaces including stone, textiles, leather and paper, the spray repels water and prevents any dirt from sticking. It is only half as good at repelling water as a lotus leaf, however.

Lotus leaves are covered in tiny water-repelling particles

Materials – food for thought

Future technologies have a way of confounding prediction. The successful insights of visionaries such as da Vinci or H. G. Wells can only be separated from the chaff with hindsight. Some trends are clear, however.

Regardless of whether the materials of the future are renewable or non-renewable, we need to find ways to make our use of them more efficient and less wasteful. The key to efficiency will lie in innovation in design, and the greatest advances will come from learning lessons from living organisms and communities who have been evolving and developing their designs for thousands of years. Plants may become as important as materials to us in the twenty-first century as they were to our earliest ancestors.

Out of Eden

It is impossible for this book, as it is impossible for the Eden Project itself, to focus just on the products, goods and services that the natural world provides for us, as if these could be separated from our spiritual and cultural existence. Woven through the stories of plants and crops too are the stories of the people who work the land for us and who deliver resources to our doors, and of those who struggle to conserve the diversity of life, so that the future does not become a poorer place. The more you look, the more you realize that the world is full of such people, their work given even more meaning by the fact that they support our most basic needs.

How strange it is, therefore, that as a society we show so little interest in what they do, or even in understanding and exploring our world, and instead are so easily bewitched by distractions such as tales of sexual and financial indiscretions of politicians and pop stars.

The obvious explanation, that we have become divorced in daily life from the processes of food production and care of the land, seems too glib. In many ways, when you have given complete trust in your own survival to others, there is even more reason to be interested in what goes on.

Of course one reason not to think too much about the state of the world is that there is a lot of worrying stuff going on. Following the ebb and flow of global life is like looking over the sea as rain clouds and sun interplay – patterns and colours form that are almost indescribable, certainly unnameable, and all simultaneously shining with light and yet full of brooding darkness. Never before have we had such a rich understanding of the other organisms with which we share the Earth, and of what they do for us. Yet we also live in a time when we seem to find it almost impossible to reduce the rate of their destruction. Never before has there been such unprecedented food security and diversity of choice for so many of us. Yet we also live in a time of greater desperation amongst farmers than ever seen before, more worries of destruc-

tive technologies, and greater erosion of the range of food plants likely to survive in to the next century.

Worse, perhaps, than these problems is a sense of powerlessness and lack of control. Who is it that makes the choices that lead to such undesirable outcomes? Is there anything that individuals can do?

There is certainly a lot of nonsense spoken about personal choice and personal action. The supermarkets' drive to find ever cheaper food, in ever more bizarre formulations, carried from greater and greater distances, is often attributed to consumer demand; but no one stood in the aisles and shouted, 'I don't care if it's January, I want fresh strawberries, and while you're at it, I want fourteen different types of cheese cracker and water from Canada and cat food with vegetable nuggets ... and don't forget the salt-and-vinegar-flavoured peanuts, and make it cheap.'

We are an acquisitive species, and want to collect shiny entertainments and luxuries when they are presented to us, but really the driver for supplying such products is not consumer demand but competition, between brands and companies and countries, tied to ever more subtle and aggressive marketing to persuade us that we want them.

When people are actually asked what they want in their lives, they do not want more 'stuff'. Overwhelmingly they wish for stronger, healthier, happier communities and the security of a world with fewer injustices. Yet in our polarized world, where many have no livelihood, many feel trapped in lives in which jobs get tougher, more stressful and competitive, and the pace and the need to travel constantly increase, and in which they scramble to make our organizations and companies more successful and competitive, producing cheaper and often surreally unnecessary goods and services for others to buy. Companies do this because standing still means collapse, and growth is the only way of surviving. We do it because, paradoxically, while luxuries have become cheap and standards of living are often all that we

want, the fundamentals such as a secure home can only be afforded by carrying huge debt that we have to stay ahead of.

Even the richest governments are in thrall to the same debt problem – providing overseas aid, even debt relief, for the poorest countries but simultaneously driving forward aggressive trade programmes and policies that make it almost impossible for small countries to make real economic progress.

So who does make these choices? Probably no one. The characteristics of the world we see emerge from the vast frenzy of human activity. They are determined by the economic and political rules of engagement, but are not predicted or controlled by economists or politicians.

So what is it that individuals can do, and what do we want people to take away from this book, and from Eden?

Perhaps the simplest and yet most important idea is to think about your connections – the huge network of people that support you. Today the farmers that keep you fed are more likely to be a thousand miles away than in the next village. And the 'community' that supports you is more than just people: it includes the web of other species that keep the world healthy and productive. As Aldo Leopold puts it, 'We abuse land because we regard it as a commodity belonging to us. When we see land as a community to which we belong, we may begin to use it with love and respect.' We need to look more to the world around us, explore it more, understand it more, celebrate its wonders and love it more.

Connections is the underlying theme of this book and also of the exhibits at the Eden Project. Every turn and very new vista is a reminder of the ways that the variety of life, including people across the world, touches us daily and needs our respect.

And if our love and respect grow, we hope there will also be a growing wish to give something back, to sustain the world that sustains us. There is currently a fixation in the environment movement on 'minimizing footprints' – reducing energy use, reducing waste, etc. – and these are all vitally important steps. But if all we do is minimize ourselves, disengage, we miss a much larger challenge. The world today needs more than treading lightly, it needs positive solutions to the riddle of how we feed the world's population and lift people out of basic poverty without wrecking the environment that we depend on. Our future is about minimizing our negative footprint, but also about having the biggest possible positive footprint, as individuals and societies, and if we learn how to do this we really can hope to leave the world better than we found it.

The encouraging side of this picture is that small changes in how we engage could lead to radical changes overall. The debt-driven international trade scramble is remarkably recent in human terms, driven by policies and decisions made just a short time ago and there are countless alternative models of how to trade, such as promoting complementary money systems not based on debt, that we can find in our own history as well as in other cultures. New approaches are always possible and we can still learn how to make our economic and trade systems work better.

Changing the world is not a difficult thing. In fact to think that change is not possible is to think like King Canute – that the world is ever

changing, and it is not in our control to stop it. The question is whether we have the wit and ability to influence change for the better. History has shown us that single ideas can influence human history at a global level, and also that small individual actions can add up to significant change, but the answer to the challenge to individual action is that we have to recognize the limits of what we can do alone. Real change also means working through the political system, not necessarily directly but by creating a social climate that encourages governments to take brave steps at national and international levels.

If, again, we look to the natural world for guidance, we can learn the obvious lesson that most organisms do not survive through competition alone: they also rely on co-operation and collaboration. This is something that has only relatively recently been well understood by natural scientists and the ideas arising from it are revolutionizing how we understand evolution and ecology. Finding a way to run our trading and economic systems as wealth-generating mechanisms that are fuelled by co-operation and conservation rather than competition and consumption may be the most important test of our civilization.

As well as introducing people to the diversity of the world that supports us, Eden's aim is to demonstrate how we can work to create the kind of world we all want to live in. Yes, there are many difficult challenges ahead and there is no guarantee of a happy future for all of us, but we have a duty to hope and find positive paths. On our site we started by showing that regeneration was possible – by transforming the pit. Having set the stage we then started to make connections to the wider world and show some of the positive environmental and social initiatives going on out there, including the story of our own successes, and failures. One thing we have learnt: working together, we can achieve far more than the sum of our parts...

Come and visit, and if you've been already come again and continue the journey.

Credits

Text credits

Editors: Mike Petty, Dr Jo Readman

with contributions from:

Mike Andrews, Angie Bromley, Harry Gilbertson, Gus Grand, Sue Hill, Dr Mark Johnston, Dr Tony Kendle, Nigel Larkin, Ian Martin, Sue Minter, Don Murray, Dr Andrew Ormerod, Georgina Pearman, Justine Quinn, Dr Jo Readman, Carla Wentink and all members of the Eden team without whose collaborative efforts this book could not have been written.

The publishers would like to thank Jo Goldsworthy and Anne Asquith for their editorial input.

Designed by Charlie Webster

Photo credits

All photographs are by Edward Parker/Images Everything Ltd, with the following exceptions:

The Eden Project: pages 8, 14b, 23br, 33, 36l, 49, 56, 63, 72, 93 inset, 104 all, 108r, 118b, 119, 128, 129, 142, 153t, 194, 195, 198, 211 215br
Bob Berry: pages 21, 174
Charles Francis: pages 16/17, 24l, 26, 66, 144, 192b, 215t, 240
Gendall Design Group: map on page 12
Future Harvest Centres: pages 69, 71, 84, 132, 136
Robert Gruver: page 221b
Richard Kalina: pages 2/3, 18, 19, 20, 22, 37r, 38l, 45, 93 main, 124, 140, 177, 192t, 205, 212b, 229, 235
Chris Knowles/Tamsyn Williams: page 187
Robin Lock: page 130
Sophia Milligan: page 230
NASA: page 30
NASA/GSFC: page 163
Nebraska Statewide Arboretum: page 143l
Jo Readman: page 46
Steve Tanner: pages 13, 24r, 25 all, 27
Claire Travers: page 14t
Charlie Webster: pages 60t, 189t, 189b

Apex: Nick Gregory: pages 23tl, 184; Tim Cuff page 23bl

Corbis: pages 48 Les Pickett/Papilio; 57+58 Martin Harvey; 101 Ed Young; 107 Owaki-Kulla; 113 John Heseltine; 134 Shepard Sherbell; 141 Reuters; 145 Gideon Mendel; 146 Phil Schermeister; 153c Julio Donoso/Sygma; 154 John Heseltine; 160 James Marshall; 178/9 David Sailors

USDA/ARS: pages 42r Scott Bauer; 80, 83t Keith Weller; 86, 88 Scott Bauer; 97 David Nance; 162 Jack Dykinga; 173, 201, 209, 213, 215tl Scott Bauer

WHO/P Viriot: pages 122, 123, 170

235

Index